With Whom Shall I Talk
In the Dead of Night

S. AMJAD HUSSAIN

THE UNIVERSITY OF TOLEDO PRESS
TOLEDO, OHIO

The University of Toledo Press

Copyright © 2012 by
The University of Toledo Press

With Whom Shall I Talk In The Dead of Night

ISBN: 978-0-932259-16-5

Book design by Stephanie Delo
Project assistance by Caitlin McCallum and Marjorie Miskey

Book title from "Snow Angel," by Satyapal Anand

www.utoledopress.com

DEDICATION

Dedicated to my children Tasha, Qarie, and Monie,
who have been my anchors in the uncharted waters
of grief and uncertainties.

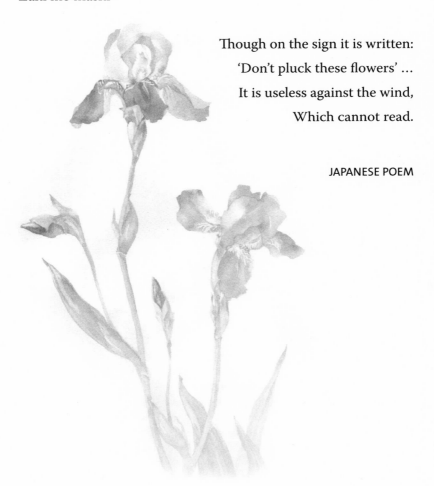

"Kono hana wa
Kataku oru-na to
Iu tate-fuda mo,
Yomenukazi ni wa
Zahi mo mashi"

Though on the sign it is written:
'Don't pluck these flowers' …
It is useless against the wind,
Which cannot read.

JAPANESE POEM

TABLE OF CONTENTS

PREFACE .... *iii*

MAP OF PAKISTAN.. *vii*

WITH WHOM SHALL I TALK.. 1

EPILOGUE.. 155

COLUMNS PUBLISHED IN THE BLADE.......................... 165

DOTTIE'S CHILDREN REMEMBER THEIR MOTHER...................... 173

A SHARED NARRATIVE 179

TERMS USED 219

A NOTE ABOUT THE AUTHOR..................................... 223

INDEX OF NAMES 227

PREFACE

Dottie, my wife and life partner of thirty-eight years, died in the winter of 2006. The past six years have been eventful to say the least.

Healing takes many paths, some conventional and others unconventional. It is hard to tell when the pain of separation and the accompanying lament and longing starts to abate and gentle breezes and warm sunshine of pleasant memories begin to enter what was, until then, a dark and scary place of the mind.

People have described the period following a spouse's death in variable terms. Some say it is like being hit by a lightning bolt, even though not many people survive a lightning bolt. Some compare this experience to being thrown into an ocean in the midst of a raging storm. Still others describe it as being pushed down into the blackest of the black corners of one's mind. All are true … but to a degree.

I like the metaphor of being adrift on an ocean of grief in the wake of a tempest that has torn away the sails and tossed away the anchor. In such situations, it is the uncertainty of our ability to weather the storm that pushes us to find an easy way out of the turmoil, letting the currents take us right to the precipice. The hard thing is to fight back, keep one's sanity and try to cobble together a life from the shards of what once was and is no more. There is always a sunrise after a scary and nightmarish storm.

Fighting these demons alone is not easy. I count my blessings that in those uncertain and dark days I had the physical and emotional support of my children and a few close friends. I think I came out of the ordeal mostly intact and whole.

My eldest child Natasha (Tasha) has always been mature and wise beyond her years. Her mother's death devastated her in a way that only daughters can understand. She not only coped with her own personal loss in a mature and graceful way but also assumed the reassuring role of family matriarch to her brothers and me.

Waqaar (Qarie), my middle child, is an actor and is extremely sensitive. In 1994, he went to London to study theater at the Royal Academy of Dramatic Art and after finishing his studies, he stayed. While in London, he relied heavily on his mother for support and counsel. They used to talk on the phone several times a week. Though we all were affected by Dottie's passing, he took it the hardest. She was his confidant and his anchor and he felt helpless and rudderless when she died. He had made frequent transatlantic trips when she was ill and arrived just in time before she passed away.

Our youngest, Osman (Monie), had his own special relationship with her. He has lived in Newport Beach, California since 1999 but has been coming home every four to six weeks. In a way he reminds me of myself and my siblings who always tried to come back to the homestead located in the old walled city of Peshawar.

During his travels within America and also abroad, Monie would always call his mother and catch up. Flying from Orange County Airport to the East Coast, he would often change planes in Minneapolis. He would grab a cup of coffee, go to a secluded corner and call his mother. Since her death, any stop over in Minneapolis unleashed a torrent of memories for him. Like Qarie, Monie also made it back to Toledo in time to see his mother before she fell into her final sleep.

And then there is Hannah [Engler], Tasha's first born. She was literally the apple of her Nano's (grandmother in my mother tongue Hindko) eyes. Since her birth Hannah had spent a part of her day at our home and the practice continued until Dottie's death. Theirs was a special bond and naturally we were concerned. She was only ten at the time but she coped with her Nano's loss with understanding and fortitude and continues to mature into a graceful and wholesome young lady.

In the book I mention Naveed and Rehana Ahmed. They were our closest friends. Their support during Dottie's illness and after her passing has been of immense help to my children and me. They are the epitome of what true friends are supposed to be.

Dottie's brother Ed Brown and his wife Barbara, and Dottie's younger sister Dr. Kimberley Brown and her husband Tony Glinke stood by us in ways that were of great pleasure and pride. We remain close.

———————————————

The idea of writing letters to Dottie came to me serendipitously during a prayer service at the Toledo mosque I attend. It was a few weeks after her passing and I was in a kind of frame of mind where the usual anchors of religion, community, family and friendships start to appear tenuous and weak. I was there mostly out of habit rather than with a fervent prayer in my heart. I was angry because despite my fervent and heartfelt prayers during her illness, the outcome remained predictable and dismal.

In that climate of uncertainty, an idea came to me from nowhere that I should start writing to her as if she had gone on a long trip. Perhaps it was an attempt to divert my attention from the minefield of doubt and disbelief. For two years I wrote to her from likely and unlikely places— parks, airplanes, mountain hikes and my favorite chair in my bedroom —to share with her what was happening in my life after her passing and also to reaffirm my love to her. It was soothing and healing.

The decision to publish these letters was not an easy one. How do you share some of the most private and intimate thoughts and incidents with total strangers? While my children were ambivalent, some of my friends thought I should publish them. They were very persuasive. I put a lot of weight on the recommendation of Samir Abu-Absi, The University of Toledo (UT) professor emeritus, and UT Professor Tom Barden. As Professor Barden put it, it is a love story and needed to be shared with others. Professor Abu Absi expressed similar sentiments. For their personal interest in the project, I remain grateful. I am also indebted to Molly Schiever who did a great job in the final editing of the manuscript, which includes list of terms and places.

Last but not least, I owe a debt of gratitude to Barbara Delventhal, my friend and confidant and also my secretary and office manager during my days as a practicing surgeon. She transcribed the manuscript while shedding tears of grief for a woman she knew well. Despite the emotional burden I imposed on her, she was able to give my hand-written manuscript a coherent shape as she had done for the twenty years we worked together.

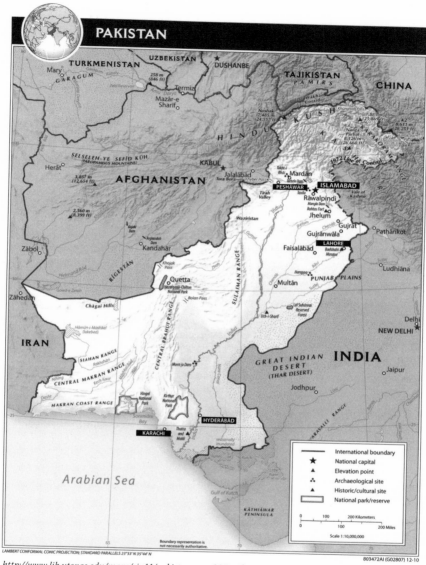

PAKISTAN

http://www.lib.utexas.edu/maps/cia11/pakistan_sm_2011.gif

With Whom Shall I Talk
In the Dead of Night

DECEMBER 16, 2006

My Dearest Dottie,

Now who would have ever thought of writing a letter to a dead person? No, I am not going crazy. I am just lonely. Even with a house full of people, I feel pangs of extreme loneliness bordering on despondency.

I am sitting in my favorite perch in the living room. I keep imagining you would step out of the study any minute as you have always done. When I do not hear your footsteps in the study, I get up and go to the bedroom, as I did a zillion times this past year, to make sure you are still in bed and that you are OK.

It has been fourteen days since our separation. I am going through the emotional roller coaster where at times I feel you have been gone a long time and then in an instant I refuse to accept that you are gone for good. I do cry and the shedding of tears makes me feel a bit better.

I don't know what happens to a person when he or she dies. Is there a heaven or hell? Is there a wayside station where people gather (I am imaging a gigantic Ellis Island) and wait to be processed or is it all a mirage and our fate is no different than the fate of other living things? I can't imagine a hereafter for animals or plants.

When I was barely seven years old, Aapa, my mother told me that on the Day of Judgment everyone would have to answer for him or herself. I could grasp that much. Then she added that on that day people will not be able to recognize each other. I asked if she would also not recognize me on the Day of Judgment. She said no and instantly I felt vulnerable and abandoned. How could she, I reasoned, my own mother not recognize me? That night I cried and the thought of being abandoned dominated my thoughts for many years to come.

So, if there is an afterlife, and I do at some level believe there is, try real hard to recognize me when I get there. I know I will be looking for you. Just give me your signature smile, press my shoulder and everything will be OK, even when the celestial police are watching.

The three sliding doors in the pit are now replaced and they look very good. Dick Hayden and his crew worked the whole weekend and installed the remaining two doors. Of course you had seen the new door in the kitchen. You were very pleased how it looked and worked. Now the job is complete. The new countertops, the doors and refurbished cabinets make the kitchen come alive. It was your project, and it is sad you are not around to see it completed just as you had envisioned it.

I wrote my column for today's paper about you, and the response has been overwhelming. The first e-mail came at 6:30 a.m., and there were at least thirty more e-mails within the course of the day, including a very beautiful note from John Block, the publisher of The Blade. I know all this attention makes you cringe. With mock annoyance, you are asking why I have pushed you into the limelight. Writing about you and baring my tortured soul was hard, indeed very hard, but I had to do it. No other subject interested me and if I had written about something else, it would have been not from the heart and not with my usual conviction.

Your story is extraordinary, and it had to be told in my own words. After all, it is my space on the Op-Ed page and I decide what I want to talk about. So today I stood on my little soapbox and talked about my soulmate and my best friend. I would have loved to see your reaction after you read it. Instead of your usual comment, "Honey, it is beautiful," you would have asked, "Why did you do this?"

As you know, a long time ago I stopped discussing my column ideas with you. Always proper and always a lady, you would talk me out of writing about certain controversial subjects because it might hurt or anger someone. I decided it was better for both of us if you saw my column only after it was published.

Everyone is worried about me (and I am sure you would be, too). They want me to start getting busy, or to put it more bluntly, to start forgetting you. I tell them I will have to go through the process of healing at my own pace and on my own terms. No one has the answer to my dilemma; they can only imagine. I don't need to escape from the reality. I need to grieve for you in private and also with our children.

I am sleeping well now with the help of a sleeping pill at bedtime. When I don't take the medication my mind goes crazy, dreaming bizarre dreams of loss and lament. But when I woke up in the middle of the night, I would cover my face with your "chemotherapy hat" or a piece of your clothing and let your lingering fragrance help me fall asleep again. We have shared this bed for thirty-eight years, and it is hard to wake up and not find you happily snoring by my side.

Just remember I love you and always will.
Amjad

DECEMBER 21, 2006

My Dearest Dottie,

It seems hard to believe you have been gone almost three weeks.
I still feel your presence in the house. While stepping into the study
I still look, perhaps out of habit, to see if you are sitting on the sofa
by the lamp reading one of your favorite books. In the closet, I still get
a faint whiff of your fragrance. Then I realize that part of it is probably
my imagination. After all, if you were around you would not leave
the clutter in the pit and in the study unattended. Sorry for letting
things slide.

Dr. Razi Rafeeq and his wife Shahida came last night. They brought
Hyderabadi food, lots of it. We sat by the fireplace in the living room
enjoying food and talking about you. It was mostly pleasant and upbeat.

Their daughter Asma's wedding went very well. I know how much you
wanted to attend the wedding and even told me just a few days before
you left that you needed to get better for the wedding. Well, our dear
friend Naveed Ahmed filled in for me as the master of ceremonies.
Somehow the word has gotten around that the inevitable had
happened at our home. Naveed didn't tell anyone and conducted the
program as if nothing had happened; still, the hushed whispers had a
dampening effect on the otherwise very festive evening.

Many people stopped by our home after the wedding. Some of the
visitors would have surprised you; but knowing you, we would have
greeted them with open arms and a wide smile. I tried to do the same
as best as I could. Dr. Mahjabeen Islam and her mother were there,
too. So were Jafar and Trish [Shah] from Chicago. Mahjabeen wrote a
very moving piece on the Internet about you. I made copies and gave
them to some of our friends. Let me quote from this brief piece.

A TRIBUTE TO SERENITY

*Some of us are known by our multiple traits. Others by only one.
Dottie Hussain stands out in my memory as serenity personified.*

*I remember the very first time that I saw her and how struck I was by her
almost perfect face, her translucent skin and most of all, her demeanor. She
carried herself with a grace that was regal. And with the dapper good looks
of Amjad, they were quite the couple. My mother said so aptly: "The couple
always emanated peace and love."*

*Friends and family had traveled from across the nation for her surprise 60th
birthday a couple years ago. Colleagues from her early years of work were
there, too.*

*And it is not really her death, but that of all who mourn her. The one who
dies is delivered, the survivors must deal with the endless taskmaster this life
can be.*

*That cancer, that terrible thief, could take her from our midst at such a young
age is numbing to me. And yet, as her life was a fulfilled and productive
one, her passage to the other world can be called a "quality death." She had
Thanksgiving dinner with her family and, as the angry scourge took a hold of
her body, hospice rose to the occasion and managed her pain seamlessly.*

*As the disease got angrier, she guessed that Christmas would not be celebrated
in the flesh. The oldest son, Waqar, works in London and was to arrive at
6:30 p.m. She knew her time was near. In and out of consciousness, she kept
verifying the time. He came, and she hugged all the family. And then with the
serenity that typified her life, she showed us that one can waltz into the next
one with amazing grace.*

*With love and a heavy heart,
Mahjabeen Islam*

I have often wondered about the threshold which one crosses to go to the other side. In the tribute, it seems one would just drift off from one level of consciousness to another. Now let me be a bit of a scientific sleuth and try to understand the interplay of forces that were going on in your body and maybe in your mind.

You lapsed into a deep sleep after you had a brief tearful meeting with us. Our son, Qarie, had just arrived from London and Monie, our youngest, had come a few hours earlier from California. You wanted to sit up, and I helped you. Then you wanted to stand up, and as you did, you wrapped your arms around me and whispered, "I love you." You sat down on the edge of the bed and put your arms around all of us—Tasha, Qarie, Monie, and Hannah [Tasha's daughter]—and kissed us and with a sly smile said, "You guys are something" (your signature quote when you were pleased with something the kids had done for you) and then you drifted off to sleep.

Our dear friend Alaf Khan and his son, Bahram, drove eight hours from Kentucky to see you. You opened your eyes, gave them a faint smile of recognition and drifted off again. From then on it was hard to arouse you. Was that the waltzing across the threshold? I know very high levels of calcium were causing havoc on your brain. That wonderful chemical we can't live without, but can't live with when it is too much. I think your cancer, that contemptible thief, started producing hormones, which leached calcium from your bones and released it in your blood stream. There were other chemicals as well helping you waltz. Your body was losing potassium in such a way that we could not replace it fast enough. God only knows what else was going on.

But between all the comings and goings you slept serenely and we could see you slowly but surely drifting away. Even Hannah's embrace, kisses and soft talk when she lay in bed with you could not penetrate the fog that now separated you from us. It was just a matter of time and that moment arrived on Saturday, December 2, at 5:30 p.m.

I had spent the previous night with you in bed. Just as you had told Dr. Kewal Mahajan, our friend and family physician prior to discharge from the hospital, that you wanted to come home and sleep in your own bed with me. That night I would escape from the awful reality and would drift off to sleep but would wake up to face the inevitable. I would talk to you, hold you, kiss you and shed tears of grief and helplessness. I would give you another boost of morphine if I saw from your face the pangs of pain, and you would fall asleep again. It was a tiring, but precious time. Each time I pushed the morphine button, I hesitated a bit, questioning myself: am I hurrying the process? Am I helping you waltz across that unknown and unknowable terrain with yet another shove of morphine?

When the time came we were with you, all of us including our nephew Pinchi [Suhail Nazir] and his wife Humaira. We all cried together and lamented together. I held you in my arms for the longest time. The kids asked if I wanted to be alone with you. I said no. My love for you was not something I hid from others; neither would I hide my agony of losing you.

That night, the boys and I lifted you off the bed and put you on the funeral home stretcher. After the van drove away from the driveway, we sat in the living room for the longest time talking about our lives and yours. We laughed and we cried. Amidst such a loss there was strength, and there was understanding that we would be all right.

Well I must close for now. I don't know where you are at this time. I don't even know if your waltz has ended or you are still in motion. I don't know if your papers to enter heaven or hell have been processed? Unless there is a big snafu or (as you would say in your most private moment, a f___ up), you should be in heaven. Is there a different heaven for different faiths? If there is, then please go over at your convenience to the Muslim heaven and say hello to my mother Aapa, that wonderful lady from the Peshawar neighborhood of Meena Bazaar, who loved you so much and to whom you reciprocated that

over. And yes, to your father Al Brown, who used
_ganized religion is just a notch below organized crime.
.. nat is he up to?

Your loving Amjad

DECEMBER 22, 2006

My Dearest Dottie,

Today's mail brought a surprise letter from a retired Lutheran pastor
who lives here in Maumee. He had read my column about you. He
had also heard that the service we had for you at the funeral home
was beautiful. He wanted to know more about you. (The spotlight
you avoided and rather hated all your life is now on you. So go ahead
and cringe if you want to). I sent him copies of various tributes which
were written in your honor. I also sent him a copy of the funeral
services program.

I was determined to have a mixed religious service for you. You
were more understanding of different faiths than most people I know.
It was an uplifting service.

Keeping in the same spirit, we had a prayer service last night at
home. (Yes, the carpets did get stained a bit with traffic and spillage
of food.) You would have been proud of our daughter Tasha and
our dear friend Rehana who prepared the house for the occasion.
We had about eighty people representing many faiths. There were
the Chablanis and their two children Raj and Alisha, Blair Grubb
and his wife Barbara, and Sukhwinder Gill and his wife Satwant.
Many people couldn't come because of the holiday season and also
because there was a wedding in the community. Those who came

sat in the yellow room (I know now why we didn't put furniture in the room for thirty years) and read from their scriptures. After the silent reading, I said a few words and asked Blair Grubb, Lachu Chablani and Sukhwinder Gill to say a few words from their Jewish, Hindu and Sikh traditions. Yehia Shousher, the elder statesman of the Muslim and Arab communities, also spoke and made some heartfelt comments. He was all emotions and very sincere. Then everyone had food prepared by Rehana, Abida Khan, and a few other ladies. I tell you, girl, a very uplifting and enjoyable evening.

Hannah was at her father's, but came for a few hours to join us in prayers. Naveed and Rehana stayed back and we, the boys and I, had a good time with them.

My sleep is getting better, but I still have to take Ambien at bedtime. I hope I will be able to stop taking it after my Pakistan trip next week.

I have decided to visit Peshawar (your "beloved Peshawar" as you used to say) to spend some time with the family. We will have fortieth day prayers for you in Peshawar. It is going to be different this time. A lot of people have been visiting the family in Peshawar to pay their condolences. It will start all over again. However, I keep thinking that it will be the first time I would not be calling you from Peshawar every day.

We don't have a Christmas tree this year. It was not a conscious decision. I wanted to have one, but when I went to get one last week, the trees from the Heatherdowns Eastgate lot were gone. I tried other places, but since it was so close to Christmas, I had no luck. I wanted a fully decorated tree in the home when people came for the prayer service yesterday. Now we will go over to Tasha's this evening and open gifts. In the morning, however, we will have brunch at Tasha's and celebrate Hannah's birthday. I gave her a writing desk from both of us for her room. It is not here yet, but it is beautiful.

I was not in a mood to do Christmas shopping. "Am I ever in a mood for shopping?" you ask. But I made a visit to Franklin Park Mall and bought gift certificates.

I am still not getting into a routine. Each time I try, I get frustrated. How do you rewrite the daily script to replace the one that we had practiced all these years?

In the morning, after I have my first cup of flavored coffee, I walk to the kitchen from the study to prime the pot with half-regular/half-decaf coffee for you. I usually catch myself and stop.

I am still, unconsciously, turning the showerhead to your favorite position, after I finish my shower. The next day, I dial it back to mine.

When I am watching TV at night, I still keep the bedroom door closed, as I had done for years, so you could sleep.

There are a million other things that have marked my days with you. Frankly, I would still want to do some of them, not out of habit, but out of love for you. You would understand, but I doubt others would.

Incidentally, while leaving home I do glance at the dining room window from the end of the driveway, just in case I might see you waving as you had done all those years.

Good-bye for now,

Your loving husband
Amjad

DECEMBER 25, 2006

My Dearest Dottie,

These past two days have been difficult for all of us. This is the first holiday without you. We had an invitation to visit your sister Kim for Christmas dinner, but we begged off.

Tasha and her family came on Christmas Eve and stayed the night. Monie grilled your favorite chicken, and we all ate by the fireplace in the living room. All through the evening, though we acted normal, joked and laughed, we did that with a heavy heart. Thank heavens for little Kevin [Tasha's son] who does know how to liven up the place.

I visited the cemetery in the afternoon. I knelt by the fresh dirt and cried. I talked to you as if you were sitting by me and listening. As I look back at my apparently silly acts of saying good night to you every night, talking to you in the cemetery and waving to an empty window, I wonder if there is much difference between sanity and the lack thereof. I know I do cross the line of rationality now and then, but this is my way to connect. I think of it just the way you used to talk to me and I would have my head buried in the newspaper. After a while I would look up and you would be gone. It is almost the reversal of roles now. I talk to an empty void and don't get any response.

Your children are still carrying on the tradition of reading "The Night Before Christmas." I am sure the three of them got Hannah to join them in the reading of the story.

It was warm on Christmas day with temperatures in the low 60s. It reminded me of the time we were in Peshawar during Christmas. It was bone-chilling cold in Peshawar, but in Toledo it was balmy and people had opened their windows.

We exchanged gifts late morning. I made breakfast, your favorite, omelet and beef sausages. Then we opened our gifts. I probably told you already I didn't have the strength to figure out what I should buy for the kids. Instead I got them gift certificates, except Hannah for whom we had bought the special gift of a writing desk.

Tasha had probably told you that we should consider giving her a desk. Well, Tasha found this beautiful desk and ordered it. It will be delivered after the holidays. This is from both of us for Hannah. She was very pleased.

Poor Hannah had to contend with another death within a week of your departure. Jeni Engler's father died. He and his wife had come to your visitation and he looked rather healthy and robust as he always did. It was a heart attack, we heard. Hannah spent time at the funeral home with her dad's family. At least she had Jeni's children there to keep her occupied.

The mortgage payment on the cottage is overdue. For the life of me I can't find the book of mortgage coupons. Can you possibly just toss it on my desk when I am not around? We had the same problem with your address book. We found it finally in the study under the glass table on your side of the couch.

You know we still can't find the receipt for the doorknobs you ordered at The Andersons. Were they from The Andersons or from someplace else? Could you please let me know somehow.

My life is in tatters. I try to keep an appearance of normalcy but sometimes the façade gives way and I feel myself drifting all alone on this dark and scary ocean of grief. I realize how easy it would be to lose focus and get pulled under the depths of despair and depression. So far I am able to keep my head up.

Rest in peace, my beautiful woman. Only God knows how much I love you and miss you. (It seems He is oblivious to these small and trivial things.)

Amjad

DECEMBER 26, 2006

My Dearest Dottie,

My morning routine has not changed. I still get up around five in the morning, drink Metamucil in my Peshawari *katora* (goblet) and prime the coffee pot with flavored (flowery as you called it) coffee. I perform my morning prayers after ablution and then go to the study to check e-mails.

This morning after prayers, I had an urge to use the rosary and repeat the short prayer on each of the ninety-nine beads in the rosary. I was conflicted. Part of me said, why should I still be carrying out the ritual when it really didn't help? You remember my sister Beego had implored me last year to utter those special prayers every morning. You may not believe in the power of prayer, she said, but please do it for me! She really believed that the combined weight of our prayers would change the course of your disease. For the past two years, not only has she been offering special prayers for you, but has also been giving money to the poor and needy.

Last December when you had that terrible episode, which took away your memory for a few weeks and you ended up on a respirator for few days, Beego was beside herself. She would have hundreds of flat bread or naan distributed to the hungry, hold special prayer services at her home and have a black lamb slaughtered as an offering for your health. After you recovered, you were overwhelmed by the way our family in Pakistan had reacted to your illness. I had no choice but to get better after all those prayers, you said. The prayers did not do the trick, I said jokingly, it was the poor black lamb that did the job.

So I was feeling a bit let down when this time, the combined weight of all the prayers didn't make a difference. It was a bit of a dilemma: should I do the rosary or should I let go? Well I picked up the rosary and repeated the prayer three times on each bead, as Beego had implored me.

The phone has quieted down. It was literally ringing off the hook for the first two weeks. Calls were coming from all over, mostly from Pakistan and quite a few from England. Everyone wants me to come and visit and everyone says I will have to accept your loss because it was God's will. It must be His will but I don't understand it. He does work, however, in mysterious ways.

I am getting a bit tired of listening to the same advice over and over again. At times I have had to console the callers, which is rather funny. Kevin, our Kevin Black [Tasha's husband], told me recently that after his father's death he found himself consoling people who were beside themselves.

I am leaving for Pakistan for two weeks. I need to go for the family's sake and bring some closure there. But I am not looking forward to the emotional toll it is going to take on me. It is going to be the repetition of the whole process I went through here in Toledo: receiving visitors and mourners all hours of day and night. Add to that the wailing, crying and carrying on, and it is enough to force you to jump off a cliff (or a second story window).

Siraj is in Peshawar and Nisar will most likely come to Peshawar from England. I just might ask them to accompany me to either Nathiagali or Dir for a few days. Our friend Dr. Shuaib Ahmad has gone on pilgrimage to Mecca but he should be back in Dir while I am in Peshawar. It will do me good to spend some time outside Peshawar in their company.

Rest well and in peace.
As always yours,
Amjad

PESHAWAR, PAKISTAN
DECEMBER 29, 2006

My Dearest Dottie,

Well here I am after twenty-eight hours of travel in my (and yours) favorite city. Zubair [Ali Shah] received me at the Islamabad airport and then we drove up to Peshawar.

I had a tearful meeting with the family. When I arrived, there were a few families, distant acquaintances, visiting. I learned that every day a few people would drop in to offer their condolences. Beego and I talked for the longest time. Crying and at times laughing as we recalled events, incidents and happenings that have been part of our lives over the past forty years. Do I need to add that you are terribly missed?

Siraj and Munawar came one evening and together, we talked still more. Beego asked me if I still did the special prayers that she asked me months ago to offer in the morning. I said I did not. They did not work, so why should I continue a failed, self-delusional practice? She was disappointed but did not show it. She must have thought I was losing faith. Perhaps she is right to some extent. I am not as fervent a believer in the power of prayer as I was at one time. If prayers could alter the course of events, then God has created too many exceptions for people to exploit. Just as Einstein had said (whimsically and tongue-in-check, I am sure) that God doesn't play dice with the universe. Maybe He doesn't play dice with other things as well. A long time ago, I heard the following lines from an Urdu poem that best describe those who pin all their hopes on prayers:

Behla rahin hain appni tabiat khazaan naseeb
Daaman pe khainch ke nsqsha bahaar ka

Those whose fate is a perpetual autumn
Amuse themselves by dreaming of the spring.

Now, I must explain that autumn in Eastern poetry is an undesirable state for it heralds the end of something. On the other hand, in the West we celebrate autumn. Who are the realists? I wish I knew.

It is bitter cold here, bone-chilling cold. As you had always said, outside mild temperatures (in the 70s) have no effect on how you feel inside a room. The rooms are chilled due to the cumulative effects of the cold wave and, in the absence of central heating, we have added quilts and blankets in the bed at night.

This reminds me of our visit a few years ago, with Siraj and Munawar, to the Himalayan town of Nathiagali in northern Pakistan, at my nephew's summer home. It took us thirty-six hours to warm only the two rooms by using electric heaters and continuous burning of logs in the fireplace. We piled on so many quilts that it was hard to move in the bed or even breathe easily. Your proximity took the chill out somewhat though.

Yesterday morning I forced myself to go for early morning prayers at the neighborhood mosque. I have been remiss and reluctant to pray. As you know, I enjoy my morning prayers. When I made it to the tiny mosque, prayers were over and the place was empty. The imam was reading the Quran aloud in his room at the end of the small courtyard. After my prayers, I peeked into his room to say hello. He stopped his recitation, asked me to come in, and embraced me, as is the custom. I said I just wanted to say hello and started to leave. He asked if I would stay for a few minutes. I sat down on the floor beside him. He told me that he learned about your passage from Zahoor Awan's newspaper column and wished to offer a prayer for you.

We raised our hands and he recited a few short prayers in Arabic and wished you a peaceful afterlife. It took just a few minutes, but it was an uplifting experience. Just imagine, a young mullah in a neighborhood mosque learns about you from a newspaper column and feels obliged to offer special prayers for you because you were such a noble person. It was very moving.

Ashfaq and Zahid [Hussain], my nephews and their families, came last night to visit. As is their habit (annoying at times), they came about 11 p.m. We had a wonderful visit though. Zahid and his wife Sultana and their daughter Warda reminisced about their visit to Toledo a few years ago. We talked and laughed a lot. You know how funny and loving those two brothers are.

Well I must close this conversation now. I need to go to bed. (Some of us have to get up in the morning, ha-ha!)

You sleep well too.
Amjad

PESHAWAR, PAKISTAN
JANUARY 3, 2007

My Dearest Dottie,

As more people find out that I'm here, we have had a steady flow of
visitors. Nasim Ashraf and his wife Assela came from Islamabad.
The kids in the family were excited to meet him, not because he is a
minister in the federal government, but because he is the chairman of
the Pakistan Cricket Board.

Yesterday I went to see Jill and her husband Bakht. The Bilands have
been calling almost daily and I told them not to bother coming to the
city. Instead, I went to Hayatabad to visit them.

It was a tearful and heart-wrenching meeting. You and Jill were the
best of friends. Your friendship went back to the early 1970s when
we lived here. So we cried, and between tears, we laughed. Together
the four of us have had some wonderful times. (Just to digress a bit,
it is 6 a.m., and I am having tea in my bedroom. I have music on and
it is Dinah Washington singing our favorite, "Since I Fell For You."
I remember dancing to the song with you in the diner in Phoenix,
Arizona, to the surprise and delight of our friends Naveed and
Rehana Ahmed and one other solitary customer at that late hour. You
were embarrassed, but you were a good sport.)

Jill is doing well. She has a healthy crop of hair now. She is still
conscious of it, but I told her that her new short and curly hair
looks good and that she looked sassy. In your case, it didn't turn out
that way, but still it was good. Unlike Jill, who had just one course
of chemotherapy for her breast cancer, you had repeated courses
spanning almost three years.

She still walks with a limp. I guess it takes a while after the new hip,
but I think most of it is because of her habit of limping for so long.

Well, their son Anwar got married in Jordan. He picked a conservative girl and just let his parents know of his decision. On their way back from England last summer, Jill and Bakht stopped in Jordan and participated in the wedding. I don't think Bakht is very happy, but what can he do. Every father desires his children to marry within their culture. I think Bakht wanted Anwar to marry his cousin, but things don't always work out the way we dream for our children.

Jill was talking about when we lived in Peshawar. Those were difficult and uncertain days for us. We lived in relative poverty and through one war. Not many people know that we left the U.S. in 1970 for a life full of uncertainties in Peshawar. I don't think I ever thanked you enough for accompanying me to Peshawar. Oh, those were the days when we sold our brand new Mercedes so we could afford shelter and food. You managed the house on a shoestring budget. A job did materialize at the university after fourteen months, but then we realized that in order to live on $75 a month, what an assistant professor was paid in those days, we had to lower our standard of living. But how could you lower it any lower than we were already doing? We rented a cheaper place and started other conservations. God bless my mother Aapa, she was part of this belt-tightening. I know you lost it when Aapa asked the servant boy to climb the tree in the yard and get a basketful of flower buds. You were aghast, but soon realized that those buds, called *kachnaal*, were the gourmet version of exotic mushrooms. You told and retold that story with relish and laughter, that your mother-in-law could cook a blade of grass in such a way that it tasted wonderful. Of course the image of a little boy climbing a tree to pluck our dinner also makes a great story.

One time, we had argued about something, which I am sure was not a life-defining or earth-shattering issue. It could have been that you were still not used to our extended family dropping in unexpectedly at all hours of the day. You never got used to this peculiar Eastern tradition. Anyhow, you were so upset that you took off your ring and threw it at me. Now, that was a shocker, because you had never taken off the ring for any reason, ever. Naturally, I also got pissed off and we barely talked to each other for days.

Aapa, ever the perceptive and gracious lady, felt the tension between us. She was not interested in why we were angry at each other but had a piece of advice for me. "You should always remember," she told me, "that in this marriage, your wife has given up a lot. She has given up her country, her family, traditions, and a lot more. On the other hand you have not given up hardly anything. So when she is upset, you must remember that." Now if that is not a sage judgment, then I don't know what is.

Jill was also reminiscing about her visit to Toledo last summer when we sat on the lawn by the swing set and talked. It was Ramadan and most of us were fasting except the two of you. You both sat by the little tea table we had set on the lawn and were enjoying each other's company. She still has a vivid memory of her last visit with you and cherishes the opportunity she had to be with you. I will visit the Bilands again before I leave Peshawar.

Yesterday, I had an unexpected visitor. Dr. Nasir Azam Khan, my teacher from medical college days, just showed up at our door. The poor soul had to look for the house in many neighborhoods. The residents must have been surprised to see the well-known physician walking the alleys of old Peshawar. Anyhow, he had read in the paper that we would be receiving friends at our home on Friday afternoon. He was going out of town so he came a day earlier. We had a short, but uplifting visit. We prayed together in your memory, and he had very kind things to say about you, even though he had met you just a few times.

Now, he was the man I turned to for advice when I was coming to the United States as a bewildered young man. I was unsure if I would be able to keep a proper perspective during my stay in the U.S. Dr. Nasir is an extremely religious person, and having lived in England for his post-graduate education back in the early 1950s, he was the person I wanted to ask for advice. I wrote to him while on the Alatalia flight from London to New York. He wrote back and reassured me that if I remembered the values I was brought up with, I had no reason to worry. I have always respected and admired him and have expressed my profound gratitude to him. He has always shown great love and courtesy to me. So it was overwhelming to see him come to our door to express his condolences.

I talked to Tasha yesterday when she picked up Hannah from school. Hannah wanted to go to our home and watch TV for a while. She sat in your favorite spot in the study and spent an hour watching her favorite program. We are all trying to connect with you in our own way and that was Hannah's.

Sleep well and remember I love you.
Amjad

PESHAWAR, PAKISTAN
JANUARY 9, 2007

My Dearest Dottie,

Two days ago, we had the gathering of our family (should I not call it a clan?) and some close friends. The imam of the neighborhood mosque came with fifteen of his Quranic students. They read the entire Quran in about an hour, each one reading one part. It is a peculiar Muslim, or rather subcontinent, tradition where the Holy Book is arbitrarily split into thirty parts without any rhyme or reason and readers sit in a circle and read in silence. Very few people know Arabic, the language of the Quran. They read it for blessing.

The imam then recited some verses from the book and prayed for your salvation and the safety and prosperity of our family. Then he went ahead, as is the tradition, to include the worldwide Muslims in his prayers and also mankind. It is fortunate that, unlike during medieval times, blessings and salvation can't be bought and thus personalized. Instead it is open-ended. We do ask a lot, and it is up to the Big Guy upstairs to sort out the requests that He receives continuously. By the very nature of our requests, I am sure He has to be extremely selective in granting our wishes.

The prayers were followed by a dinner that consisted of raisin and chickpea pilaf, meatballs containing whole eggs and the ubiquitous chicken and sweet rice. Even though raisin and chickpea pilaf doesn't go with the rest of the food, it was a complete meal in itself. We did it because you loved it so much.

My cousin Waheeda [Ghafoor] came to visit. She has breast cancer, and after primary surgery, she is now relying on non-conventional treatments, rather than chemotherapy. She looks good. She gave me a poem she wrote for both of us. As you know, she writes extremely well. This Urdu poem is about companionship, loss, and cherished memories.
It is very poignant, as well as inspiring.

I think the fortieth day prayers helped me and the family to bring some sort of closure to your passage. I have, however, not felt anything has closed for me yet.

As a matter of fact, I dreamed that we had switched roles. I saw myself to be counting days, and you were consoling me. I was sitting down on a narrow couch and you sat down next to me. I asked you to lie down with me on the narrow couch, and you did. We embraced and kissed. It was a long, loving kiss. When I woke up, I had this great feeling of elation and satisfaction. I know it was a dream and dreams are but the work of our unconscious mind, but still it was real enough, and it left a lingering fragrance. So thank you for the embrace and the kiss.

You remember the large music collection that a Peshawari friend of mine, Allah Dad Khan, had collected over the past sixty years. Whenever I was in Peshawar, I would visit him and listen to my favorite songs on 78-rpm records. He died a few years ago and his family wanted to get rid of the collection. His sons have absolutely no interest in keeping the collection in the family. There are about 10,000 records, and most are in good shape. I tried to get some museum interested in acquiring the collection, but that didn't happen. Siraj and I bought it and brought it to Siraj and Munawar's home in Hyatabad.

Last night, Siraj and Munawar invited all those men who used to go to Allah Dad's home every week to listen to this music. About forty people came. Siraj acquired an old turntable, and we had a fantastic time listening to the scratchy old music. Some of it was from the 1920s and 1930s. Siraj and Munawar served us a delightful dinner. The gathering broke up around midnight.

At Siraj's home last week I met a retired university professor who was our college contemporary. He lost his wife to thyroid cancer a few years ago, but he talks about her as if it happened only recently. It was a love marriage, as the marriage of choice is known in Pakistan, and they had a good life. While listening to his story, I wondered if for some people, the ache and pain of separation ever go away. They haven't for this man. I hope I don't carry my pain and hurt as openly as he does. I don't think I loved you any less than any man could love his wife.

Let me end this letter with a small poem by Sarah Teasdale:

THE COIN

Into my heart's treasury
I slipped a coin
That time cannot take
Nor a thief purloin,

> Oh better than the minting
> Of a gold-crowned King
> Is the safe-kept memory
> Of a lovely thing.

With all my love,
Amjad

PESHAWAR, PAKISTAN
JANUARY 12, 2007

My Dearest Dottie,

I am still in Peshawar. I am getting into a lazy, extremely lazy, routine.
I get up about 5 in the morning. I laze around for a while, then go
down to the kitchen and make myself a pot of tea as I have done
whenever we came here. Next, I check my e-mail and squeeze in a few
(a lot them, in fact) games of solitaire. After I wash up, I walk to the
mosque where morning prayers start a little after 6 a.m. It has been
an uplifting experience. After breakfast, I enjoy beautiful sunshine,
read, write, and listen to music. Lunch is anytime after 2 and then I
take a nap. Evenings are usually at home in the kitchen where a pot
of glowing charcoal is placed on the floor, under the low table, and a
big, really big, quilt is placed on top of it. We sit around the low table,
put our feet under the blanket and talk until dinner, which is around
9:30 or 10 p.m. Oh, I forgot the afternoon/evening tea, which is served
in the kitchen where we all sit in *sandli*, the name for the contraption
of table, charcoal and blanket. This brings back memories of my
childhood, sitting around the sandli and eating nuts and fruits on
winter evenings.

I have gone to the Lady Reading Hospital a few times to give lectures. I really don't have anything new to offer, but they are quite content in listening to me rehash some of the old presentations that I am sure some have already heard. Well if they don't mind, why should I?

Khyber Medical College is soon to be elevated to the status of a university. There is a lot of pulling and pushing for the appointment of vice-chancellor for the new university. My name has also been suggested for the post. It is a long shot, knowing the politics of such appointments, but still it is amusing to speculate if this would come to pass. I would like the opportunity to serve in this capacity. This new institution could set the trend for higher medical education in the province and in the country. It would be wonderful if we both could do it. We had often talked about coming to Peshawar for an extended period of time every year. If this happens, it would mean a real extended visit. I have not been trying for the appointment, which in Pakistani traditions means visiting influential people and seeking their help. Since I am not looking for a job, it should be up to the powers that be to ask me if I would like to take it. Again, in Pakistan that approach doesn't work.

If I were to be given this opportunity, I would spearhead the efforts to build a sprawling complex in Hayatabad. It would have research labs, a conference center, dormitories and guesthouses. I can imagine a close academic liaison with some of the universities in the West and also with other Pakistani universities. The difficulty would be to change the culture of dependency and complacency as everyone thinks the government owes him or her something. I am confident those attitudes can be changed with a private and public partnership. My aim would be to raise the standard of medical education in the province to that of Aga Khan University Medical College in Karachi. The graduates of that college are decidedly more learned and more polished than graduates of any other medical college in the country. Stay tuned for further developments.

Shuaib is back from the Hajj and came to see me. My plans to visit with him and spend a few days in Dir didn't materialize. Ever the proper gentleman, he decided to drive down to Peshawar, a five-hour rough ride through the Dargai and Malakand passes, and then go back.

The rush of visitors has now become a trickle. Still it is rather inconvenient when people arrive unannounced to pay their respects. I know I should not be that impatient, but then I dropped Job as my middle name a long time ago.

There is a lady who was married to a well-known dentist here in Peshawar. Her husband died two years ago and according to her he died of medical negligence. He had polymyositis [an inflammatory muscle disease] but was in good health. She came to see me on the pretext that she had an urgent medical issue to discuss. What she wanted was to seek my support in her case against the physician who took care of her husband. I was rather blunt with her. I told her that she needed to decide what her objective was. Was it revenge or getting compensation? If it was only to reprimand the doctor, then that was doable. After talking to her for about an hour, I didn't know what she was trying to accomplish. It was a rather difficult and irritating meeting. She wanted to give me a minute-by-minute account of what happened and what did not happen. I think the sooner she puts this behind her, the better.

Beego's next-door neighbor, Koko Jan, talks about you a lot when she comes over for an occasional cup of tea every day. She is totally blind as you know, and she is losing her short-term memory. She would ask the same questions again and again. Poor lady! She is still charming, courteous and gracious. And it is still fun having her come over through the door on the terrace.

Abai, the servant lady—I feel embarrassed to call her "servant lady" because having spent more than thirty years in this household, she is anything but a servant and still exercises great authority, asserting it with other women who come to do the washing and cleaning—is getting crippled now due to arthritis in her ankles and feet. She can't walk comfortably and it is difficult for her to climb the stairs, which she must do a few times a day.

I enjoy my early morning visit to the neighborhood mosque. It is pleasant to be in the company of people from the neighborhood. After prayers, I stay in the mosque a little while and contemplate. I also talk to people and enjoy that very much. I will miss them when I leave for Toledo next week.

So long for now.
Yours always,
Amjad

PESHAWAR, PAKISTAN
JANUARY 16, 2007

My Dearest Dottie,

Of late I have been going over all the years we have spent together. I start at the beginning and think of the moment I saw you for the first time. You may not remember, but I do.

I was a first-year surgery resident at [the former] Maumee Valley Hospital in Toledo. One day I was in the cafeteria line, and after taking my tray, I started to walk towards the doctors' dining room. That's when I saw you. You were sitting at a table with a few of your friends. What I saw was a ravishing young woman with blonde hair and blue eyes and a very attractive face. I asked my friend Anwar Haq if he knew who you were. He said he did not. He was apparently not so impressed, but I was.

I made contact through some friends but you weren't interested. You turned me down for a date because I was dating another girl from your nursing class. Your refusal, however, did nothing to dampen my interest. But when I was able to convince you that I was not dating her anymore, you agreed. I don't remember where we went. It could have been a greasy spoon restaurant in south Toledo. There was one on South Detroit Avenue close to Glanzman Road. You were enchanting, and you were good company.

In the column I wrote after your passage, I said our love was not love at first sight. I guess it took us a year or so to realize that we were two incompatible people. But then, a genuine love and affection always help diminish incompatibility. You were a strong-willed and stubborn girl, and I was equally strong-willed and obstinate. But instead of parting company, over time, we drew closer.

Oh, I remember the spats we had! I remember this one particular conversation when I called you from the morgue where I was assigned to do autopsies. The day before, you had become rude and nasty with me in the lab where a few of the student nurses used to hang around with lab technicians and residents after work.

We talked and agreed to carry on our conversation later on in the evening. I think it was that call from the morgue that set in motion our friendship and eventual togetherness. Imagine—a conversation initiated from a morgue that led us to spend our lives together. It does not sound very romantic but that is exactly how it happened.

The bunch who worked at the lab were unique. Lacy Godwin, Tom Carrol, Jim Blanchard, Bob Haines, and others were extremely friendly, good-natured and very competent. Lacy had a big crush on you. You had always denied it, but he did. He once told me that I had stolen his girl. But I have to give it to him. He kept his feelings at bay once we got married, and I seldom felt a twinge of jealousy.

You remember the tiny house on Woodsdale Avenue in South Toledo? You moved in after our wedding. That place was the beginning of our thirty-eight-year-long journey together. Although I had a maid come every two weeks to clean the place, you didn't think she did a good job. She was good at sweeping everything under the proverbial rug. It took you weeks to put the place in shape. How I loved to come home in the evening and see you cooking dinner in the tiny kitchen. At times you wore the ankle-length terrycloth blue dress. Somehow that dress, the Woodsdale house, and that tiny kitchen are part of my memories from that time.

I am also thinking of Mrs. Sylvia Milde, who lived next door to us. She was, I believe, German or Austrian, and her husband Paul was American. They had met in Europe during World War II. Now Mrs. Milde was a kind and caring neighbor. I vividly remember the incident, and I am sure you do too because you were ready to kill me for what I did.

Our dinners were always topped off with dessert. And good, home-cooked good meals were showing up in my increasing girth. I asked you to skip the ubiquitous sweet dish that had become part of our evening meal. You agreed. The following day after dinner, I had this craving for something sweet but there was nothing in the kitchen or pantry to satisfy my craving.

Through the kitchen window, I saw Mrs. Milde at the sink in her kitchen. I opened the window and in mock anger, started complaining in a loud voice about not having dessert with my meal. You were horrified, but that did the trick. A moment later, Mrs. Milde appeared at out front door with a cake. She was a great baker and always had baked goods in her home.

Before coming to Peshawar, I drove by the house. The house is now painted purple instead of white and I think it looks awful. I stopped to look around and see if I could get permission to go inside to revisit some events of our life. But a woman in short shorts, gaudy jewelry and tattoos refused to let me in. I think she was suspicious that I was from the police.

Yesterday I took a ride to Peshawar's University Town and visited the neighborhoods where we had lived in the early 1970s. The sprawling bungalow and the spacious annex look just the same. The house brings back memories of your finding our two-year-old son Qarie unconscious in the abandoned servant quarters in the back of the house. Whether he was overcome by the smell of rotten onions piled in one room or bitten by some critter, we would never know. But we did go through hell when he remained semi-conscious for two days and was unsteady on his feet for another week. He made a full recovery, but the incident shook us to our core.

The annex on Karakul Lane, where we had lived for two years earlier, also looks the same. I didn't have the time to go to the main house and inquire about the well-being of our landlady Marge Mahmood. I have heard she has been very ill.

My stay in Peshawar is winding down. In another two days, I will leave Pakistan for home. I dread entering the home and finding it empty. After our granddaughter Hannah was born, I had written a column about her. In the piece I said that it was inconceivable how a small tiny baby can fill a big empty house. The absence of one person can have the opposite effect. I will have to face your absence with understanding and try hard to get on with my life. That is what you made me promise, and that promise I am determined to keep.

Stay in peace.
Yours,
Amjad

My Dearest Dottie,

Today I am taking a day off to chill out at home. It is a beautiful day. The sun is out and the garden on the terrace is awash in sunshine. There is not a speck of cloud in the deep blue sky. The kids in adjacent houses are on the rooftops flying kites. Why aren't they in school, you ask? Well, I don't know. An occasional flock of domesticated pigeons flies overhead and changes direction abruptly when they hear the shrill whistle of their owner in the next neighborhood. A Pakistan International plane drones above in a landing pattern heading toward the airport. It is a perfect day.

I am trying to enjoy the days and the interactions I have with people. But sometimes people get rather nosy and inquisitive.

My nephew Zubair has told me that certain members of the family (not from his household) have raised the question as to why I delayed your burial for two days. Zubair was rather blunt with them and told them to call me in America and ask. Well, no one called, but when I came here, some people looked for an opportunity to raise these questions with me.

Why was the burial delayed? (They asked this innocently but I know better.) In order to make arrangements and to give friends a chance to come, we delayed it for a few days.

Did you keep her at home all that time? No, she was in the funeral home.

Who stayed with her? No one, although we visited (Tasha and Rehana, if you must know).

But our religion says a body should never be left alone. The body is alone after burial, isn't it? So what is the difference?

Were there many people there for her funeral prayers? (This question was tricky because they wanted to know and be reassured that you had a Muslim funeral.) There were lots of people at the funeral. We had a service, but we did not have Islamic funeral prayers.

Why not? Because she was not Muslim.

This brought the conversation to an abrupt end. Ever the proper and sensitive man, I could see anger in the eyes of my nephew, as to the stupidity and insensitivity of these busybodies.

You never converted formally and that was OK with me. You gave our kids a religious and cultural identity. What else could I expect? I am sure you are better off than most of these ignorant idiots who think they have a corner on religion and salvation and who can't see farther than their ablution *lotaas*.

I have often thought about where people end up after they depart this world. It is amusing to think that for some Christians (Catholics in particular) there is a halfway house in purgatory. Jews and Muslims don't stop in the middle. They go where they are destined to go. Hindus send their souls to a giant recycling factory where their souls are reincarnated according to their deeds. If one was good, then he/she gets a better life. Otherwise, they go down the list of preferred life forms. The cycle continues until one reaches perfection or nirvana. Do you remember Suresh Ramnath telling us one time, tongue in cheek, that once he dies, he will not be recycled. He was a neurosurgeon, he said with a mischievous smile, and there is nothing that could top that.

So, if you are where everyone assumes people go after they die, then it must be a strangely unique place. Do they have different areas for different religions? If so, do people ever interact with each other? And if it is just one humongous celestial sprawl, then how do you keep track of who is who? Do people live as families in neat houses with manicured lawns, but no garbage pickup and no toilets? I would assume one doesn't need those services.

And if you have this latter arrangement, then you must have met my family—my brothers, particularly Nazir (Paaji) and my mother, Aapa. They both loved you so much, and you reciprocated their love many times over. Is Aapa Gul, my eldest sister, still bitter about life? Do your mother and father still bicker and fight? And how about Sheeda [Khursheed Begum], my fireball of a younger sister? Irrepressible, funny, full of energy, brave, brainy, at times boisterous, but full of love and giving. I miss all of them.

I hope you are able to see these people and talk to them ... as I cannot forget when my mother told me that on the day of judgment, mothers will not be able to recognize their children. That was the clincher that gave me nightmares. I lived with this trauma for many years and still do in some metaphysical sense. So you see heaven, hell, purgatory, accountability, punishment, reward, stick and carrot are still a big mumbo jumbo for me. I believe in them at some level, which is not physical or tangible.

Or, do all these boundaries and places vanish when one dies? I believe all that is left behind are the good deeds (now that is tangible) and fond memories. The atheists and agnostics worship at the altar of a godless universe, and they seem to be as comfortable as those of us who profess and follow. And if this were all true, you would still come out ahead. After all, your legacy and influence are being felt by everyone who knew you. It will be felt for a long time to come.

It is about three in the afternoon, and I am being summoned for lunch. I love you.
Amjad

PESHAWAR, PAKISTAN
JANUARY 18, 2007

My Dearest Dottie,

In just two days, I will be leaving Peshawar for home. (It still sounds right even though you will not be there to receive me with open arms as you have always done).

I had a bizarre dream last night. I dreamed that you were angry with me that I let you go without putting up a big fight. It made me angry, and we had a rather contentious argument. I know sometimes best of intentions are misconstrued and misunderstood. The dream was playing out a small disagreement you and I had just days before your passage, towards the end of your third day in the hospital. You were depressed and non-communicative. I tried to talk to you, but you were not inclined to talk. Instead you went into a deep sleep from which it was hard to arouse you. Barb and Kim were there, too.

On so many occasions before, you and I had talked about situations in which neither of us would like extraordinary measures to keep us alive when there was no hope of recovery or survival. This decision required "Do Not Resuscitate" (DNR) forms to be filled out and signed. I told the nurse that if you had a cardiac arrest during the night, it was your wish not to be resuscitated. Your doctors agreed and ordered it. As your nurse took your wrist to put the bracelet on, you asked about it. After hearing what the bracelet meant, you got very angry and upset and told the nurse you had made no such decision and had not consented to any decisions about DNR. When the nurse called and told me, I felt bad.

Later on, you lashed out at me in front of Kim and Barb, saying that the nurse brought a bracelet that meant if you had some heart rhythm problem during the night, they would let you go instead of helping you. You were acting just like your mother at that instance. I tried to explain, but to no avail.

Somewhat later that evening I apologized to you and asked for your forgiveness for making such a dumb decision without talking to you again. Half-resigned, you said you forgave me, but I had known you long enough to realize that such stains do not wash away by a mere "I am sorry" statement, even though it came from the heart.

Oh, how does one tiptoe through the minefields of doubts, suspicion and momentary distrust?

Surprisingly, you were candid with Mark Burton, the oncologist, about going home with hospice care. There was a bit of resignation on your part, but overall, you appeared to have accepted the inevitable.

Then Don Corbin, the St. Charles Hospital chaplain, came in and you told him that you were going home with hospice care. He asked you if you were comfortable with that decision and you said, "Yes." Tearfully, the three of us prayed together. You came home on Thursday, November 30, and left two days later on December 2.

I want to put some of the bitterness behind me, but it keeps surfacing. I hope it is genuine and not a sort of defense mechanism where, in my subconscious mind, I need to tarnish your wholesome image to get some reprieve from my pain.

I hope not. Though I do remember our arguments and disagreements and not talking to each other for days at a time. In one case, it was weeks, if I recall correctly. You were stubborn to the marrow of your bones, and I was stubborn in my own ridiculous way. Reason and logic don't work when people argue in anger. I guess we never learned to fight in a constructive way. On such occasions, few and rare as they were, we fueled each other's anger—you for being vocal and I for staying quiet and withdrawn.

I must admit that, at some level, I wanted you to feel some pain during those tiffs. I was also driven by my inner desire not to be hurtful. As a result, I ended up hurting both of us.

You always said that most people (including our kids) didn't see the angry side of your personality, since you made sure we didn't argue in front of others. Our kids still think we never had a fight in our married life (and they probably also think we never had sex).

At some level, I am still angry with you for abandoning me—as if you had a choice. My whole world is upside down. I am functioning at a bare minimum level. I do get frustrated and angry at the disruption of our small routines, the morning coffee, small talk in front of the TV, occasionally having lunch by the pool and so much more. When I am alone, I scream and I cry. Does that help? I don't know, but what choice do I have? In all this I also see a bit of betrayal.

Forgive me for ending this on an unpleasant note, but then perpetual happiness or a flawless life is a myth.

Stay in peace.
Amjad

MOON PALACE, CANCUN, MEXICO
FEBRUARY 1, 2007

My Dearest Dottie,

I reached home last week after a grueling thirty-hour travel. I thought
with the passage of time things would get better, but they did not.
Jet lag and fatigue appear to be more prolonged and deeper than the
last time. Naveed and Rehana came to pick me up at the airport. As
I exited customs, I glanced at the chair where surely you had waited
for me, returning from Pakistan, barely three weeks earlier. It was still
empty. Did I really expect to see you there? No I didn't, but I glanced
… just in case.

Tasha had left the lights on in the house so I wouldn't enter a dark
place. Lights did take away some of the gloom, but not really. You
were everywhere, in the living room, the study, the bedroom and in
the closet. I buried my face in your clothes and cried. I screamed, I
yelled, I called you just to vent my pent up pain, anger and frustration.
I can still smell your fragrance in some of the clothes.

Tasha had cleaned the closet in my absence. She took some of your
clothes upstairs to the cedar closet. It looked tidy and spacious.
Small consolation.

 It was difficult to adjust to a haphazard life at home. I went to the
university [The University of Toledo Medical Center], ran other
chores, read, wrote and slept. I still can't bear to turn on the TV and
do our year-old routine: 6 p.m., *BBC World News*; 6:30 p.m., *ABC
News*; 7 p.m., *Wheel of Fortune*; and 7:30 p.m., *Jeopardy*. After that
you used to watch *CSI* and I would glue myself to the computer. I
haven't watched *Little House on the Prairie*, *The Waltons*, or any of the
other old shows we would catch most evenings.

I invited Saleh Jabarin one evening for dinner. There was plenty of food in the house, and I thought we would have a relaxing time at home, which we did.

On so many occasions during those last four months, you had asked me to go out and have dinner with him. I just couldn't. To leave you home was not something I could do if I could help it. Anyhow, we had a pleasant evening that lasted four hours. We talked about the perennial topic—the Islamic Center and the Khattab Chair in Islamic Studies. We talked about you and his wife Dorothy, who had passed away two years earlier of breast cancer.

This past week in Toledo was long, but I had to catch up on so many things before leaving for the seminar in Mexico. But things got done. I finished preparing my seminar presentations and left five days ago. Most participants are old friends and acquaintances: Dee and Lance Talmage, Marcine and Jerry Marsa, Patrick McCormick, Nancie and Lachman Chablani, the Greenbergs, Lee Wealton, Bill Sternfield, and Corrine and Tom Welch. Sue and Don Marshall and Lara Thaxton and her husband Kevin are here, too, with their two little children Dawson and Morgan. Penny Reed decided not to come this year. She is still the mourning the passing of her husband Ben.

This was the first time I had seen many of them since your passage. Needless to say, most of them did not know what to say. It is really an awkward thing to find appropriate words to talk about someone's personal loss. I tried to put them at ease. They all liked the column I wrote about you. Pat McCormick remembers the day when his father passed away in Toledo. We were in St. Martin and went over to his cottage to express our sympathy. Isn't it amazing how some gestures make such a difference to some people?

Our sons decided to come to Cancun for a few days to keep me company. They might have also thought they should keep an eye on me, at least for a few days, to make sure I don't take a walk in the ocean towards the United States. We had a great time together. They fit in rather nicely in the group. One day we went to see the ancient Mayan ruins at Tulum. Monie had been there before. We rented a Jeep and drove one hour to the site. Monie, in the best rendition of American college kids, took off his shirt and drove bare-chested. You would have been horrified.

Qarie had developed a plantar wart that was causing him much difficulty in walking. On the way back from Tulum, we stopped at a pharmacy and bought a few syringes and a small bottle of sterile local anesthetic. It is strange how one can buy anything, including narcotics, without a prescription there. We could not find a surgical knife and proper sutures though. But those things did not prevent the Mayans, or any other ancient peoples, from performing surgery.

With Monie's assistance, I carried out surgery in our hotel room. Qarie's theatrics aside, it went well. The incision was made with sharp scissors,and the wart was successfully removed. The bleeding was stopped with compression and then as a safety measure, I stitched the gap using ordinary needle and thread retrieved from the sewing kit in the room. Next day, he was able to put pressure on the foot. I wanted to make sure it wouldn't bleed, just as the previous skin biopsy from his foot had bled last year. Poor chap was at Kmart when the site began to bleed. He left in a hurry, trailing blood in his path. You and I stitched the biopsy site in the garage.

Last night, we had the group dinner at the hotel. It was, as usual, a pleasant evening. You missed the gossip and other delicious tidbits that invariably come out in such settings. You were always oblivious, willfully I must add, to gossip. A good time was had by all. I also had a chance to talk to Cecilia Bennet. It has been eleven years since Al Bennet died. She is traveling a lot. She has taken three cruises around the world (at $150,000 a pop) and lives in Hilton Head. Yes, she still carries her husband's ashes with her wherever she goes. She says it was his wish, and she is happy to oblige. What a wonderfully eccentric woman she is.

It is really cold in Toledo now as winter has arrived belatedly in Ohio. Tasha told me on the phone it snowed a few days ago. She took the kids sledding on the golf course in the back of our house. I know Hannah missed you when she came in, and she did not find her hot cup of chocolate waiting for her by the fireplace.

I must close now. I am going to walk the beach and then have breakfast. No, I don't intend to walk in the ocean towards our home in Toledo.

So long, my love, rest in peace.
Amjad

Lake Diane, Camden, Michigan
February 9, 2007

My Sweet Love,

My card group had been talking about coming to the lake house for over two months. Finally, we struck upon a weekend that happened to be convenient for everyone. The seven of us—Nawaz Chaudhary, Naveed Ahmed, Bahu Shaikh, Jim Adray, Karim Zafar and Munir Ahmad—are here for a weekend of nonstop card playing interspersed with debates, discussions, and expression of strong opinions. Yes, there is a lot of smoking. In gatherings like these, those who usually do not smoke get in the swing of it for a few days. Karim is the only one who doesn't stray from the straight and narrow.

Our little hideaway is still beautiful. When we came yesterday, there was a lot of snow on the ground, and it has been very cold. The furnace works, and the water quality is good. The lake is frozen solid and yesterday, we saw some brave snowmobilers raising clouds of snow on the lake. I don't know what happened to the ducks. I didn't see any on the lake. I guess when the entire surface is frozen solid, they need to get to some open water. After all, what good is a duck without water?

We haven't seen any deer either. There are a lot of tracks in the front and back, but no deer yet. We were confounded by some tracks on the deck, which looked like deer tracks. Unless the big momma jumped over the low gate (both were closed) and then jumped out, there is no way she would have left those hoof prints. I can't think of another animal that might have left those neat, cleaved impressions in the snow.

You have always enjoyed the solitude of this place. Except for some hectic discussions that we had in the past twenty-four hours, the place is still tranquil and peaceful. Just a glance outside the window calms one down to an indescribable serenity.

Naveed and I took a walk on the long driveway (it is half a mile long, I think). Actually we went to clear the driveway of the brush and fallen branches. A few snowstorms in the past three weeks had dumped a lot of debris on the path. A large tree branch had broken off the tree and was still attached to the tree by few threadbare fibers. It was precariously hanging over the driveway. We enjoyed doing that work. I remember how at the beginning of every summer, we would walk the trail and trim the overhanging tree branches and brush to prevent them from encroaching the path. Those walks were fun, and I miss them so much.

Naveed joined me for a little grocery shopping in Camden. We stopped at the farm of our Amish friend Henry Delagrade. He invited us in, and we had coffee and homemade cookies with his wife Mary and their grown children. They were really sorry to hear that you had left us. In their own gentle way, they extended their sympathies and prayed for you.

Mrs. Delagrade was keeping their four-month-old grandson (son of Amis and Emma, the same girl whom you found milking the cow and cleaning the barn of manure just a day after her wedding). He is the most beautiful baby. You would have, as was your habit, gone gaga over that baby. Their daughter Mary is married now and lives close by. It is always a good feeling to visit these simple and down-to-earth, decent people. Emma and Amos also live in a house on Henry's property.

I have been mulling over what to do with the cottage. It was our shared refuge. None of us enjoyed being here alone. I remember a few nights I spent here alone, and I was miserable. Tasha said she would use the place this summer and have Hannah and her friends come over more often. That would be good. I am also concerned about not being able to keep the place up. It is now becoming obvious that it takes a lot of work to maintain a residence and to keep it in top shape. We men somehow don't realize the amount of work that goes into making a place look nice. I am already seeing water stains in the sink and washbasins and am at a loss as to how to remove them.

Though I am functional most of the time, occasionally I feel very uncertain and perhaps irrational. This is only when I am alone. You know I am good at suppressing my inner feelings and uncertainties, but they can be agonizing in private moments of solitude.

I love you.
Amjad

FEBRUARY 14, 2007
VALENTINE'S DAY

My Dearest Dottie,

This Valentine's Day, we had the worst weather of the decade. A blizzard hit us late last evening blanketing everything with snow and ice. Howling winds blew all night making the house moan and groan. It was not as bad as the one in 1978 but still bad enough. A level three emergency paralyzed the city and northwest Ohio.

I picked up Hannah at her dad's and took her for lunch. I haven't done that in a long time. We had a good lunch at Max & Erma's restaurant. Then we went to the florist and bought flowers for Tasha and a small bouquet for Hannah. We thought we should also get you some flowers, too. Considering that the temperature was in the minus-zero range, we didn't get fresh flowers, but had an arrangement of silk flowers affixed to an easel. (Forgive me, for I know your distaste for artificial flowers). We both went to the cemetery, where we had to trudge through shin-deep snow to get to you. We put the easel down, steadied it the best we could and wished you a happy Valentine's Day. It was sad but very comforting and satisfying.

It is a winter wonderland outside. Some snowdrifts are three feet high and have buried the patio furniture under mounds of snow. I have both fireplaces going and am enjoying the cozy comfort of a warm living room and study.

The house is in good shape but with a proviso. Just keep in mind the little marble sign the kids once gave you: "Cleanliness is Next to Impossible."

The study is cluttered, especially my desk. Somehow, papers and books keep piling up there. Your gentle reminders (and sometimes not too gentle, I must add) would force me to keep it tidy. One of these days I am going to surprise myself and clear the study. But before I do that, I will have to figure out what to do with the increasing volumes of books. They just proliferate.

... the next day (February 15)...

Tasha is in Washington this weekend. I took her and baby Kevin to the airport this morning. Her husband Kevin is already there. She will be back in three days. Hannah is at her dad's. It is really amazing how John and Tasha have kept their divorce-induced differences and bitterness to themselves and pay full attention to their daughter.

I am still having a difficult time finding things around the house. As was your habit, whenever I asked about something, you brought it and gave it to me. So I never learned where everything was. Yesterday I looked for the Pakistani *lehaaf* [quilt] and couldn't find it. It has been cold at night and I thought the quilt would add a splash of color to the bedroom, but my plan was not to be. Alternatively, I found an old afghan in the linen closet and brought it down.

We received a call from the bank about your safety deposit box. I didn't know you had a box at the bank. Tasha didn't remember it either (we later found out that she had opened the box once about fourteen years ago, but she had no recollection). The box had not been visited since 1994. Well, that created quite a stir in our family. Was there something you had placed there with the idea of us retrieving it after your passage? Were there any secrets you wanted us to know afterwards but not during your life?

Now, I didn't know that I could not just walk in the bank, show the keys and access the box. We had to go through the probate court and have me appointed administrator of this little estate of yours, only for opening up the box and then closing it for good. You can imagine as the days passed, our curiosity increased and we started referring to it as Al Capone's vault, a reference to Geraldo Rivera's dramatic opening, on live TV, of Al Capone's vault in Chicago. In the end that event was a bust as there was nothing but empty space and accumulated dirt and dust inside.

We also talked about finding a treasure trove of letters and memorabilia not unlike in *The Bridges of Madison County*. In that movie, the grown children of the character played by Meryl Streep find letters after the passing of their mother.

In our case the box was not empty, but alas, there were no intriguing tidbits. It had the jewelry that the family had bought for Tasha's wedding in 1991. Each jewelry case was marked as to whose gift it was. You were precise and efficient when it came to those things. I brought the jewelry home. Tasha wants it to be distributed among her brothers and Hannah. We will do that when everyone gets home next week.

Qarie will be here in five days and Monie is coming the next day. Monie will spend four days here. Qarie goes back to London after spending two weeks at home. It will be good to have them home. It gets awfully lonely here without you. Sometimes, in my naiveté, I walk into the study expecting you to be sitting at the end of the couch by the lamp reading a book. Reality sinks in when I don't see you there, and reality can be, as you know, very cruel and painful.

Dr. John Howard, that country southern gentleman, was talking about you the other day at the university. He always thought the world of you and always inquires as to how I am doing. I remember when I used to ask him the same question when his beloved Nina died a few years ago. He used to tell me it is awfully lonely without her. Two years after Nina's passing in 2000, he met his and Nina's college friend Sara Sheppard Rice, and they got married. He is so happy now. He told me he and Sara visit Nina's grave every week.

Rehana's sister Susie and her niece Saadia are here from Ottawa, Canada. Naveed's sister and her family from New Jersey were also supposed to come, but bad weather prevented them. Susie and Saadia came and visited me yesterday afternoon. Last night, I went over to Naveed and Rehana's for dinner. Imran Alis and Noor Pirzada were also there. It was good seeing all of them after the lapse of two months.

Rest well my Billo.
I love you.
Amjad

FEBRUARY 25, 2007

My Dear Dottie,

During the day, I go through the motions of living a life with a semblance of normalcy. I think of hundreds of things I want to tell you and many incidents I want to share with you. But when I pick up the pen and paper, somehow those thoughts evade me and they evaporate. I need to start jotting down notes as those thoughts come to me. I can't recall things at will the way I used to, and I think in recent months, I have lost a few more neurons and synopses in my brain.

It is also becoming evident that tasks committed to memory do not always get recorded in my head. I have to write them down. Would you believe I forgot to take Hannah to school this morning? She waited an extra 10 minutes before calling me. She is punctual like her mother and you, and is quite uncomfortable when people are late. Well, I got her to school on time after all. I just will have to start writing notes and reminders to myself. If only I could keep track of where I put down those damn notes.

Monie stayed a few days and has gone back. Qarie goes back to London next week. Coming home has been particularly hard for Qarie. Last night, he was in the garage playing the guitar and felt an uncontrollable need to see you and talk to you. You both had a wonderful bond when you would join him for a smoke in the garage and would talk for long periods of time.

He came in from the garage, and we talked. Then he came over and sat down on the couch with me, put his head on my chest, and cried. We both did. We held each other and just let our inner turmoil come out through streams of tears.

We now have Dottie Hussain's distinguished lectureship at the College of Nursing at The University of Toledo. Every year, a nationally distinguished nurse will be invited to come to Toledo to give lectures on clinical nursing to students and community nurses. The first of these lectures will be held in April, just six weeks from now. I know you would be embarrassed to have your name in the limelight, but we thought it was a fitting tribute to you and your passion for the profession of nursing.

Last week, I met an Austrian man in New York. What was I doing in New York? Well, it was the second anniversary of our dear friend Johar Mir's death. There was a literary gathering in his memory and we unveiled a special edition of the literary magazine, *Zaavia*, that he used to publish from New York. The publication ceased after he passed away. Atiq Siddiqui, Irshad, and I have decided to foot the bill for this commemorative issue to celebrate Mir's life and his works. Irshad did a fabulous job of collecting and editing the material. There is so much love for Johar Mir in New York literary circles (and elsewhere in this country) that it overwhelms me. It was a great event. Atiq came from upstate New York, where he now runs a bigger hotel. Irshad Siddiqui came from New Mexico and stayed with me in my hotel room.

I mentioned the Austrian man and then got sidetracked. Anyhow, I met this man who is from Austria and surprise of all surprises, he had worked at the famous hotel on Kaiser Franz-Josephs-Höhe Glacier. Boy, just the mention of that hotel brought back a flood of wonderful memories.

Our friends Joe and Ann O'Leary had suggested that on our trip to Austria, we should try to go to the hotel overlooking the glacier. They had trekked the glacier and stayed at the hotel on one of their hiking trips. It was, Joe said, one of the most memorable places they had visited.

Our own side trip to the glacier was full of surprises. The first came when we tried to enter the toll road that winds and climbs up the Grossglockner Mountain. We were told that the weather was bad, and we would have to wait. It was funny because there was a beautiful sunshine that afternoon and not a speck of cloud could be found in the blue sky. After an hour or so, they let us enter but warned us to be extra careful because of bad weather.

Within half an hour of driving up the mountain, we realized the weather had started to turn foul. And the snow started to fall. As we climbed, the wind and snow picked up, and we had to drive ever so slowly. Now we were really afraid. A small Frito-Lay truck was ahead of us and we followed in its tracks. There was absolutely no traffic on the road. In this blinding storm, we drove for another hour or so until we saw a sign for the hotel on top of the pass. We left the main road and followed the signs another mile to the hotel.

First, I thought we had stumbled upon an abandoned property because the parking lot was empty and there was absolutely no activity anywhere. The hotel, a stately wooden structure, appeared empty and forlorn. But as we entered the lobby, a smiling and enthusiastic staff greeted us. They were surprised that we were able to come because the road had been closed for many hours. They were expecting a couple hundred guests that evening, but now we were the only guests in the hotel.

The dinner was a long, pleasant and memorable experience. Instead of telling us the time dinner would be served, they asked us when would we like to dine. I still remember the big window by our table overlooking the massive glacier. Then we retired to our cozy spacious room with all the charm of an old and bygone Europe, canopied beds with fluffy comforters, cotton slippers, bathrobes and claw-legged bathtub with a view of the glacier. It was a romantic night of unprecedented dimensions. We would often talk about our stay there with approving nods and sly smiles.

Things were different in the morning when we went down for breakfast. The charming solitude of the night before was gone and was replaced with boisterous noise of many busloads of tourists. We had breakfast and then made a hurried exit.

It is hard to believe it has been three months since I held you in my arms and said a reluctant and tearful farewell.

You are not coming back, are you?
With all my love,
Amjad

MARCH 9, 2007

My Dearest Dottie,

The past week has been difficult for me to say the least. I thought with the passage of time (it has been three months now), things would start to settle and one would feel some measure of relief. Instead it has been a slow simmer, no outburst, just a quiet storm under the surface, as I have mentioned before.

At times, I want to lash out, scream, kick and punch. It is a combination of anger and grief a realization that there is not a damn thing I can do to change things or to settle things.

I am going through the motions of having a normal life, but the appearance is just that, an appearance (I am good at it, as you were). I know I need to do something to get myself settled down a bit.

My current beneath-the-surface turmoil reminds me of the turmoil
Hawkeye Pierce went through in one episode of *M*A*S*H*, where
Hawkeye suppressed his feelings and tried to act normal—his usual
wise cracking self—but couldn't. It was the psychiatrist, Sydney
Freedman, who helped him verbalize his suppressed memory. A
Korean woman had deliberately suffocated her baby in order not to
draw the attention of the enemy soldiers when Hawkeye was traveling
with a group in a bus. The baby was whimpering and everyone was
scared that the soldiers would hear the baby and come for him or her.
I am not suppressing my memory, but the storm under the surface
keeps tormenting me. I have had thoughts of taking the easy way out,
but the very idea of taking my life repels me.

One time we argued about your being not attentive enough to my
physical needs. I had said (you never forgave me for that even though
you made fun of me later) that I could have everything done, by hiring
someone. I can't and will not hire someone for my physical needs. The
same is true now as it was when I spoke those words in the heat of the
moment. I need your physical touch, embrace, a loving kiss. The rest
should be easy, but it is not.

This morning I sewed buttons on a few shirts and a cardigan. It took
me some time to locate and find the sewing box. As I sat in the living
room trying to sew on the buttons, I realized that you would have
done them without my even realizing a button was missing from a
shirt cuff or collar.

The weather is changing. I think I can smell the faint fragrance of
spring in the air. There are underground stirrings of renewal and
rejuvenation. It is always a special time of the year. After a long dark
winter, when life seems to come to a standstill, spring heralds a new
beginning. The snow is melting, the birds are back and soon we will
see tiny buds bursting through the hard crust of tree branches.

Ron Cowie came for the weekend to attend Maumee Valley Country
Day School's Board of Trustees meeting. He takes his appointment on

the board rather seriously. It was good for Qarie that Ron came. The only thing is that both of them leave a trail of dirty dishes, half empty cans of pop and mud tracks in their wake. It is good that I am short-sighted.

Enough for now.
Yours as always,
Amjad

MARCH 18, 2007

My Dearest Dottie,

I am at the end of a miserable week. You were on my mind this whole past week. Lord knows how many times I broke down and cried. It didn't take much to trigger an emotional downpour of tears. I am surprised it doesn't happen more often given the fact that your reminders surround me.

Qarie left a week ago. He had been here for the last three months. He came just the day before you left us. I will never forget the tearful reunion you had with him and Monie and the rest of us that evening.

I took Alaf Khan and his family to the cemetery last Saturday. I found Qarie at the gravesite. When Alaf and his family left, we both hugged and cried. We needed that. Qarie had been there for an hour and, as he told me, he had been talking to you through tears. Somehow the bonds you created with the rest of us are as strong and fresh now as they ever were.

Your life insurance is going to pay $100,000. It will have to be distributed to the three kids according to the estate plan. The children have decided to use the money as a down payment for an apartment in London. It will free Qarie from renting in London, and he could pay his rent towards the mortgage. I am deeply touched by this gesture of Tasha and Monie towards their brother. It will help Qarie develop some equity while working in London.

I still have not been able to get into a routine. Frankly, I still don't know where everything is. A few nights back I couldn't stop coughing. Cough medicine just did not work. I thought that the air was too dry and that was irritating my already irritated throat. I searched the whole house but couldn't find a humidifier. We did have one, I remember, but in the middle of the night I couldn't find it. The next day I bought a new one. I am having the same problem locating other stuff–clothes, propane, fire starters, matches and what not. When I used to ask for something you always got it for me, even though I would offer to fetch it. But you knew how careless I am, and it was easier for you to get it than to tell me the location. Aapa used to tell me that I had buttons for eyes. You would tease me and call me "button eyes" whenever I gave up locating something–which was usually there in plain sight.

If you are in heaven, give Aapa my love. You both loved each other, and I would love to see both of you communicating with each other. Do you still speak with her in a mixture of English and Hindko, or is there some other language, which is common currency in the hereafter? I will never know unless you tell me.

We have started a new tradition in your memory. Sometime ago, Tasha bought a number of small pewter turtles, just the size of thumbnails. We are to carry our turtles wherever we go as a reminder of our love for you. Qarie lost his, and Tasha replaced it. (I think she knew how her father and brother are, so she bought extras). Monie sent a picture of his motorbike with turtle taped to the handlebars. I carry my turtle in my pants pocket and so far, I have been lucky and have not lost it. Kevin and Hannah also have their own turtles.

Did I tell you that The University of Toledo invited me to deliver the commencement address in early May 2007? It is a singular honor and I feel flattered to be asked. Oh, how I wish you were here so I could bounce ideas off you. You have been my inspiration and my critic. I miss that very much. It reminds me of the time, some twenty-five years ago, when I was preparing my talks for my visit to Pakistan. We both went in the study and told the kids to leave us alone, so I could rehearse in front of you. A physician called for me and Tasha told him I was giving a lecture to her mom. Later when I saw that physician, he remarked that all men should lecture their wives once in a while. When I told him the kind of lecture I was giving you, he was amused.

It has been not quite four months since you left us. I still meet people who have not heard about your passage and ask me about your well-being. When I tell them, they feel awful for asking such a question. Every week I meet one or two persons who were unaware of your illness.

Little Kevin is two years old. He has just started to say a few words. His favorite word is Nana. He is growing up fast and getting smarter every day. Tasha and Kevin were concerned about him not talking by this time. She took him to Dr. Vijay Adappa and his ENT (ear, nose and throat) checkup was normal. So was his audiogram. I think he is going to be OK. He is a normal kid and is a bit tardy in speaking.

Recently, I came across a stack of letters that we wrote to each other. One dated March 10, 1972, you wrote to me when I was still in Peshawar and you had returned to the United States with the children. Let me write a few lines from that letter. It is prophetic, but in a reverse way.

> My Darling Amjad,
> It has been so long since I've received a letter from you. I am half out of my mind with worry. Have you written and they have just not come through or what?
>
> I am to the point where I think of you constantly. I dream of you nearly every night, of being near you and actually touching you. A feeling of emptiness is ever present. It has been three months that we have been apart.

I can't say it in better words. I still imagine you are next to me in bed. I still say good night to you and try to caress your back, as I did every night.

Rest well and rest in peace.
I love you.
Amjad

MARCH 26, 2007

My Dearest Dottie,

You have been on my mind a little more than usual these past few days. Elizabeth Edwards, the wife of Democratic presidential hopeful, John Edwards, has had a recurrence of her breast cancer. She had a mastectomy two years ago and was told she was disease free. A fractured rib, unrelated to her cancer, led to the diagnosis of recurrence in lung and ribs. Then the clichés started flying. It was said that cancer is not curable, but it is treatable. It was said that she might go a long time before cancer claims her life.

I couldn't help recalling the clichés the physicians used in your case. Towards the end of your illness, I was getting tired of your oncologist saying that it is not the length of time, but the quality of time. I am sure you, too, disapproved of those euphemisms for death. It meant only one thing—there is not much we can do or offer. I remember him saying we may not be able to add more years to your life, but we can add more life to your remaining years. How? Do they know that the ravages of chemotherapy diminish life to the point where the remaining years and the quality of life both shrink to the point of a continuous exercise in futility?

Maybe these clichés and euphemisms work for some, but I know for sure they didn't work for us. Now Elizabeth Edwards is going through the same play of words that create unrealistic expectations in a dire situation.

They have decided that his quest for presidential nomination should continue. She is going to campaign for her husband as much as she can. They have young children, six and eight years old, and one older daughter. I question in my mind the wisdom of continuing this relentless pursuit of the presidential nomination in the face of this horrible personal situation.

Looking back, I was very pleased with my decision to retire a few years ago. It gave me time to be with you and do mundane things that brought so much joy to us: our morning coffee together (yours half regular/half decaffeinated; mine, hazelnut decaffeinated with an equal measure of regular coffee) and my fixing a breakfast of omelet, toast and fruits. There was the occasional lunch of fresh French bread, spread with cheeses, meats and relishes, and served with fruits and an occasional glass of forbidden nectar. Your cancer didn't go away, but we tried to make the best of a bad situation.

You were always in a hurry to leave just before three in the afternoon to pick up Hannah from school. This was something you wouldn't trade for anything. This was in reality, the highlight of your day and Hannah's, too. You would bring her home where she would sit in the study on her favorite chair and have her snack in front of the television. Then you would spend an hour or so helping her with her homework. After that, during the finale of your quality time, you two played cards or a board game for a half-hour or so. I marveled at the bond the two of you had developed and at times, I felt left out. But it was your time together, and I admired it.

A few weeks ago, Lachman Chablani and I did a case presentation at St. Charles Hospital's Continuing Medical Education weekly conference. It was about a young woman with ovarian cancer. I discussed the case with the attendees to generate some discussion about various possibilities. They range from benign and innocent causes to the sinister and fatal conditions. As I discussed the case, I kept thinking why couldn't you have had a benign condition, rather than a condition that took you away? Frankly, I do get angry sometimes at the unfairness of this Russian roulette, but anger doesn't get me anywhere. I have come to terms with it and try to sort my life from the debris of this terrible wreck.

I am struggling to add a few new fixtures to our home. I am averse to changing everything and giving the home a new look because then, it wouldn't be the same. The change would take away the soothing comfort, along with the lingering pain. This dilemma reminds me of a character in Salman Rushdie's *The Satanic Verses*, where after the death of a spouse, the house is maintained in the same era time-warp. The curtains, the furniture, the clothes, the utensils, the automobiles are just the same, frozen in time, but still being used on a day-to-day basis. Is it a lingering wish that one day the front door may fling open and a departed spouse may appear/materialize? I have thought about that myself. Frankly, if I could see you, I would have the shock of my life. But every so often, my loving mind gets ahead of my rational mind, and I hear voices and feel a presence around the house.

So I am trying to change things here and there, but in a subtle way. Maybe it is my way of getting rid of the clutter around me. The books have appeared on the coffee table and are encroaching on the space by the fireplace. Since you are not here to remind me (no, the proper word would be to nag me) to take care of the clutter, it tends to get that way.

Spring is here, I think. Except for the daily temperature's wide swings, the weather has changed. No buds on the trees yet and no flowers in the flowerbeds, but I can hear them stirring. It won't be long.

The pool is scheduled to open in late May, and Hannah is already planning to use it more often this year. I might also try to get in the pool a time or two myself. Last year I did not use it even one time. Somehow our moonlight swims, rare as they were, seem so remote and distant.

Just know that we all love you and will love you to the end of our days.
Amjad

APRIL 1, 2007

My Dearest Dottie,

Tomorrow it will be four months since we lost you. It has not gotten any better. The lament, the void, the pain, and a feeling of being adrift are still there, but not as intense or overwhelming as it was a few months ago.

For the past six to eight weeks, I have been hearing strange noises around the house. These might be just structural creaking of the house. After all, spring is here and the house responds and adjusts to climatic change. Last night I heard the distinct sound of you clearing your throat. Over the years, I had become used to it and could hear it from anywhere in the house. I hurried back to the bedroom and found nothing. Other times, I have heard footsteps, but again they might be explained by physical laws of nature. Then again, may be I did hear something that was uniquely yours.

A long time ago, I read an essay by Carl Sagan, of the "billions and billions" fame and host of the PBS *Cosmos* series. He wrote about alien abductions ... you know how people claim alien spaceships had abducted them and they heard the voices of their long departed relatives. Mr. Sagan said that because we have heard certain voices over and over during our lifetime, it is not strange that a particular voice would reverberate in our mind's ear, if something triggered and stimulated certain parts of our brains. Was my mind playing tricks on me? I don't know. Mr. Sagan's reasoning has another implication: perhaps in our brains there are recorded sound tracks of the voices, and the images of people, places and events long past.

Maybe we can have a replay of those sounds and images. Pray tell, where is the rewind button?

I am not giving into fantasizing about the hereafter. In one of my previous letters, I said that I really do not believe in a physical afterlife. That does put me in the quandary of only looking back at the time we have spent together, with nothing to expect in the afterlife.

During their lives, many people promise their loved ones to contact them from the other side, but none has done that. Even the great trickster and illusionist Houdini, despite his promise, did not deliver. So, I am inclined to believe that once you die, you die for good. Is it true? Are we then left only with a permanent record of memories in the end? Can we have another person's soul embedded in our psyche? Yes, one can, according to Douglas Hofstadler, a professor of cognitive science at Indiana University. He lost his wife in 1993 in a car accident, and he believes her soul lives within him. The original is gone, he says, but a less detailed and somewhat coarse-grained copy remains.

I don't understand all this scientific jargon (mumbo jumbo to some), but can say that four months later, I still feel your presence in my life and in my heart. And it is not less detailed and coarse-grained either. It is in sharp focus like a high-resolution scan.

April is the month when we got married in 1968. It brings back vivid memories of our friendship, courtship, and our decision to get married. It must have been the fall of 1967 when we decided that. At the time, you lived in the Sawicki apartments on Michigan Avenue in Maumee. We took a walk on the sidewalk and discussed the pros and cons of getting married. I must admit, I was extremely nervous to make a commitment, but I did. We decided to get married in April.

I passed by the apartment a few weeks ago. It is amazing how certain events and places are etched in the mind forever. And I told you that I also passed by the tiny house on Woodsdale Avenue where we lived for three months after our wedding. Instead of white, the exterior is now painted in a gaudy green. It was ugly even to a partially color-blind person like me. A bizarre thought came that I should stop and give the owners money to repaint the house white. I don't think they would have taken kindly to some stranger asking them to repaint the house to satisfy one's nostalgic yearning for the past.

Thinking of the past and Woodsdale, I heard from our friend Imtiaz Butt in Vancouver, British Columbia, a few weeks ago. I had shared that house with him and our other friend Rifaat Hussain.

Imtiaz found out rather late about you and called me. He cried as we talked. He has not been in good health. He has been living with a low-grade, small-bowel obstruction for the past many years. Not only was Imtiaz a good friend, but also he is the one who lost a bet and had to buy our wedding rings. While we were housemates, we use to egg each other on to get married. At the time, he was dating a beautiful nurse from the hospital. Then we made a promise to each other: Whoever gets married first will have the other pay for the wedding rings.

After our walk by your apartment in the fall of 1967, I called Imtiaz in London and reminded him of our pact. True to his word, he sent me the money and we bought simple gold bands, which we have worn ever since. Mine is still on my finger, and yours is now with Tasha who plans to give it to Hannah to make a necklace. (Isn't it amazing that during all these years I worked and every day had to take off my ring to perform surgeries, I never once lost it.)

The other Woodsdale resident, Rifaat Hussain, is being his usual stubborn and eccentric self. He must have heard about you from his brother, but has not bothered to call or write to me. You always had a soft spot in your heart for him and used to defend him whenever I complained about him. Somehow you accepted his eccentricities that I never could. Friendship, like any relationship, is a two-way street. It may be difficult for some people to meet halfway, and I would accept that, but to expect a friendship on only one's own skewed terms is just not acceptable to me. I am sure he has his own reasons that I am not aware of.

I have been picking up Hannah from school sometimes. She is always eager to come to Nano's home after school and have a snack. Today, I brought her home and cut up some fruit for her. She wanted some peanut butter for her apple slices and for the life of me, I couldn't find a jar. During the renovation of the kitchen, many things got thrown out. I realized that I have not been stocking food that might be of interest to others. How selfish of me to live a spartan life and not think of others. We have not had iced tea for the past four months. Well, I made a pitcher of peach tea for Hannah. And now it is here, I will also drink it.

Telemarketers have stopped calling. They always asked for you. Most of them apologize when I tell them of your passage, but some are persistent in peddling their wares. One particular satellite company called again and asked for you, though on previous occasions I had told them of your passage. This time I gave them the address of the Highland Memorial Gardens, but cautioned them, since you don't have a telephone, to only write to you. They are persistent, if nothing else.

There is a lot more I want to tell you, but will do it some other time. With all my love,
Amjad

1968 wedding photo of Dorothy Brown and Amjad Hussain.

Honeymoon, near Tampa, Florida. Playing checkers on the beach.

1968, a few months after wedding.

Greenfield Village, with Tasha. 1969.

A rare lunch on the steps of the apartment. Tasha is in the stroller. 1969.

Peshawar. Dottie with Tasha and Aapa, Amjad's mother.

Dottie with Tasha. Peshawar 1971.

At the feet of one giant Buddha statue at Bamiyan, Afghanistan, 1972. The Taliban destroyed two ancient statues honoring the Buddha in March, 2001.

Lock Haven, Pennsylvania. Amjad, Dottie and Monie.

Camping Pokagon State Park, 1978.

Dottie with Midwest Medical
Mission in Dominican Republic 1988.

Portrait 2004.

With
grand-
daughter
Hannah
2002.

With Qarie 1998.

Amjad with Monie (on Amjad's right), Tasha and Qarie two years after after Dottie's
passing 2008.

APRIL 10, 2007

Dearest Dottie,

It is past 11 p.m. After doing laundry and watering the plants, I just sat down. The place looks a bit cluttered, but I have no desire to keep tidying it up. I just do the big, obvious stuff; small detailed cleaning is beyond me. Tasha tells me that I am keeping the house looking nice and that is good enough, even if she says those things to please me. I will just have to remember the sign the kids bought for you and you put it in the kitchen—"cleanliness is next to impossible."

You will be pleased to know that I am now getting into a routine. Taking my shirts to Threadmill Cleaners, running an occasional load in the washing machine, tidying up the kitchen before going to bed, etc. Of course each of these steps remind me of you. Actually, there is not a single moment I don't think of you.

I have stopped playing squash as of now because of pain in my right shoulder. This is the same shoulder I injured in that fall from my bike two years ago. Sometimes, squash aggravates it. It is frustrating when I have to rest the shoulder by not playing squash. I have been neglecting it for the past many months in the hope that it will get better by itself. I saw a shoulder expert at UTMC today. He injected the shoulder and asked me to start physical therapy for six to eight weeks. I hope this takes care of it. I don't want to have surgery on my shoulder. I am sure many people benefit from shoulder surgery, but a few people I know have really gotten worse after surgery. If these measures do not succeed, I will have to say a very reluctant goodbye to my beloved squash.

I have also started yoga classes. A lady gives one-hour yoga lessons at Sunforest Court in Toledo every Tuesday morning. Last Tuesday was my second visit. I am still trying to concentrate on my breathing. Breathing is automatic, and we are programmed to do it from the moment we are born.

Yoga requires you to concentrate on breathing. I try but it is hard. My mind drifts off in a thousand different directions. It is not the breathing but the shoulder pain that brings me back to reality.

Speaking of squash, last weekend Saeed Zafar and I went to Denver to see Hashim Khan, the all-time-great squash player. He is ninety-three and still sprightly. His wife, however, is very ill, and has been in the hospital for many weeks. She has undergone amputation of both legs and is on respiratory support. At eight-four, she still looks great but was not able to identify us. She is in a coma and there is no hope of her ever getting better.

Hashim talked at length about you. He said you were one-of-a-kind and that he had not seen such an American married to a Pakistani who played the role of wife so beautifully. How could one not agree with him? He was overwhelmed that Saeed and I would make a daylong trip just to say hello. I was also pleased that I got a chance to enjoy Saeed's company. We had dinner one evening and it was just beautiful. We talked about many things, but of course, we talked about you. Saeed loved you dearly and you loved him too. There was a beautiful chemistry between the two of you. So over a prolonged three-hour meal, we reminisced and talked.

Incidentally, he is doing very well. He has regained his strength and his spark. I think the awful collagen vascular disease is finally behind him. Did he go through a baptism of fire or what? He damn near died, but he is now back to his good old self. It was a pleasure to spend a day with him.

Hard to believe, but true, spring has finally arrived. Temperatures have been in the high 60s and mid 70s. The grass looks good and we have already had two mowings.

Two weeks ago, when I came home, I saw that the lawn was mowed. The only way I could tell was that the two white chairs from the back yard had been moved. I had left two chairs on the lawn since the visit of Jill and Bakht Biland last fall, after a picnic in the back yard. Well, not really a picnic, because it was Ramadan and most of us were fasting, with the exception of you and Jill.

You were surprised when I brought the two of you a tea tray. It was a lovely afternoon. That evening we talked and said that it was too bad that we didn't use the backyard more often. Perhaps as a reminder of what we had talked about, I'd left the chairs on the lawn rather than bringing them to the deck. Removing those chairs from the backyard signals, in a bizarre way, that life must go on. There is no permanence to anything, I guess.

In this era of fast communications, you would think that almost all of our friends and acquaintances would have heard about your passing. To my surprise, I am still getting calls four and a half months later from people who somehow did not learn of it at the time. Instead of consoling me, I end up consoling them.

Yours as always,
Amjad

APRIL 20, 2007

My Dearest Dottie,

It was our thirty-ninth wedding anniversary today. True to my intractable habit of forgetfulness and superimposing dates, I had to be reminded by our daughter that the date is not 4-18, but 4-20. Forgetting is not something new or startling, for I have done it so many times in the past. On many occasions, my office manager Barb would remind me when I got to the office. That wonderful lady thought so much of us that she always tried to keep things smoothed out between us.

I wrote a letter to our children on this occasion. It was something I wanted to share with them. After all, they have been part of us, and I wished to tell them the deep love we had for each other. It has been said that the best gift a father can give to his children is to love their mother. Here is what I wrote:

My Dearest Tasha, Qarie & Monie:
(It does sound like a single name to me)

April 18, 2007 is just around the corner. We would have observed our thirty-ninth wedding anniversary on that day.

It doesn't feel like that long ago, when your Mom and I, in the winter of 1967, decided to get married. I was leaving Toledo for Detroit in July of 1968, to start my residency at Wayne State University. Your Mom was afraid that once I left Toledo, I would not look back. I guess she did not know me that well. We took a walk on Michigan Avenue in Maumee (by the turnpike overpass) outside her apartment. That walk and the talk sealed our fate for the next thirty-eight years.

For me, it was to take the pleasant with the unpleasant that life deals us all. I must admit that at times it was difficult, but we never strayed away from our main focus of caring for each other and for the three of you.

I got to know her more during her illness. She was all giving and didn't really expect much in return. (Now that does not take into consideration her few quirks/habits that I attributed to having been inherited from her side of the family).

We both agonized during her illness. At times, she was OK with it; at other times, she was not. She kept a brave face to everyone, including the three of you. She would only show her agony to me and sometimes she would hide it from me also. Oh, how I wished and prayed that I could switch places with her.

Ours was a unique relationship. She cared deeply for my side of the family and I appreciated that and told her repeatedly. And I reciprocated. As you all know, I was very fond of her parents and also of her siblings.

At times I am amazed at our story. Here are two people, who had nothing in common, except their love for each other and their commitment to their children. And yet they lived a life of contentment, some would say a charmed life.

I miss her as you all do. I am grateful for having you. You three are the embodiment of your mother and you constantly remind me how good and unique she was.

With all my love,
Dad

Of late, I have been reading and trying to understand the life-after-death concept. All religions point towards an afterlife and every religion has given it a color and tone that is in sync with the beliefs of that faith. What is blissful existence, what is reward and punishment, and more than that, what is the meaning of life? Such philosophical musings can get one lost in the maze of religion and philosophy.

Blessed are those who take life as it comes and are grateful for whatever it brings. These people are smart and wise, because they know and accept that there is really no choice or alternative.

I continue to feel your presence at home. Perhaps my imagination gets the best of me, but I swear I saw an impression on your side of the bed, as if someone had just sat there and left tell tale signs on the bed spread. I told you in a previous letter that I have been hearing noises, which are unfamiliar to me. Last night, I heard knocks upstairs. I was in the living room reading and heard soft tapping, as if someone were knocking on the bedroom wall. The surprising thing is that in the past, I would have been anxious and a bit apprehensive, but now I am not jittery when I hear noises. I smile and accept them, whether they come as a result of an explainable physical phenomenon or a friendly and loving knock from the other side. Hey girl, are you trying to tell me something?

Last week I gave a talk at The University of Toledo as part of a symposium on religion, philosophy and medicine. My topic was interesting: "Can prayers alter the inevitable?" Naturally I chose the topic in the light of my own life experiences. I don't think prayers can change the outcome, no matter how fervently we pray.

You remember the time when I was on pilgrimage to Mecca and you called to relay a message from our friends Attia and Mahboob to offer a special prayer for his little girl who had a brain tumor? I did, but the inevitable happened anyway. I don't think God changes the events he has set in motion. Five years ago, the so-called benign and innocuous borderline ovarian tumor started in your pelvis. Who knows if the never-ending cycles of chemotherapy made any difference, either immediately or in the long run? The inevitable happened. If we had done nothing, would the outcome been any different? Some times I bog down with these what-ifs but I try not to. When the ethereal world of religion comes in contact with the hard-science world of medicine, one cannot escape the all enveloping, and at times suffocating, dust storms of doubts and uncertainties.

This morning Dr. Ben Pansky, emeritus professor of anatomy, stopped by my office. This courtly and genial gentleman lost his wife two years ago to pancreatic cancer. They had been married fifty years, and it was barely a month from the time of her diagnosis to her death. He is still bedeviled with the doubts and what-ifs that become part of our narrative when we lose a spouse. We talked for a while, realizing that we have a shared story. He is a remarkable man. He has written more than half a dozen children's books and authored a book of anatomy that has gone through six editions in English, and several in other languages. Such people, as you know, have always inspired me.

Earlier I was talking about voices and knocks from the other side. During our seminar on philosophy and medicine, I briefly discussed the work of the well-known psychiatrist Elizabeth Kübler-Ross, who in 1969, published her seminal work on death and dying. In later years, I have read, she started dabbling in the afterlife and claimed to have communicated with deceased people. Was she getting crazy? Or had she stumbled on an as-yet-undiscovered or unexplored dimension where one could go from here into the hereafter and then return to tell the story? Sort of what Christopher Reeve did in the movie *Somewhere in Time*.

A few weeks ago, I went to Ann Arbor to visit Dr. Munib Rahman. You remember him and his Swiss wife Zeba. They had visited us on many occasions. She was a linguist and they lived in Aligarh, India for seventeen years, where they taught at Aligarh Muslim University. She died two years ago, and the man was devastated at losing her after fifty years of marriage. He has gone blind, but can manage living alone. Actually he insisted I come for dinner, which he cooked himself.

It was so wonderful and uplifting to visit this great man of letters and to listen to his poetry — some romantic, some nostalgic, and some full of lament. Here is rough English translation of one Urdu poem he recited for me that he wrote in memory of his wife:

You are starting a journey on an unfamiliar path
The destination unknown
I hold your hand to stop you from leaving
Alas, my efforts do not succeed.

A voice inside my heart keeps saying
It is too dark outside
Please don't go
Please do not venture into the unknown.

My soul and my body will long for you
The pain of separation will ever be etched on my face.
My inner turmoil will always be there
*   in the never-ending rain of tears*
Who would, if not you, lift the crushing burden,
*   from my heart?*

We both are helpless, trapped and destined
Who could hear the silent lament of my love and longing?

How cruel and lifeless is this dark night?

How apt. How true and how pertinent!
Yours as always,
Amjad

APRIL 26, 2007

My Dearest Dottie,

After a gorgeous few days, the weather has turned again to a wet, clammy, and depressing state. The pewter sky drips, like mist, gently and cautiously. But I want a thunderous roar and a torrential downpour. I guess this weather might lift some spirits, but not mine. I desperately need some sunshine and some warmth to sooth my aching soul. Today I need someone to lean on just as in the Bill Withers' 1972 song:

> *Lean on me …*
> *We all need somebody to lean on …*
> *Call me if you need a friend …*

The last two years of your life it was your favorite refrain. You used to say that more and more … you lean on me. On days like today, I feel like going to sleep and not waking up. Which reminds me of the funny phrase you guys used in the emergency room when some one was found dead in the morning: He woke up dead. Perhaps you meant the person did wake up, but in some other realm.

A lot has been happening here in Toledo and on the home front. Last week there was a concert held in Way Library in Perrysburg, sponsored by the Karen Morley Khan Music Fund. The fund was established by Nasr Khan, his family, and his Perrysburg friends. The Khan brothers were there and so was Maureen, Karen's daughter, and her husband, and Bill Morley and his wife. It was good to see them.

You continue to receive phone calls, and I politely tell them what has happened. Most of them are very understanding except the occasional telemarketer. The most difficult calls are from some creditors. A few days ago someone called from Massachusetts and asked to speak to you. I informed them that you were no longer with us. She went on to tell me that you owed an outstanding lab bill. It seems they still have not credited the payment made for the lab work that Imran Ali, your neurologist, had ordered in December of 2006. I told her that it had been paid; she promised to look into it and call me back. That was a week ago, and she has not called back. Next time when someone calls and asks for you, I am going to give them the forwarding address at the cemetery.

Arshad Rehan came from Columbus a few days ago and spent a few hours with me. Sara and the kids are doing well. In March, they all went to Pakistan for a month as Anwar, Sara's brother, came from Jordan with his bride. Bakht and Jill Biland gave a large dinner to celebrate their son's marriage. You remember that I told you Anwar has married an extremely conservative Arab girl from Jordan. She observes complete seclusion and even Arshad was not allowed to see her or meet her.

Anwar has always leaned towards extreme orthodoxy and he has found a wife who matches his outlook. Sara and Anwar are siblings, but they are so different from one another. Who is to say Sara is not a "good" Muslim? To me, she is not only a very good Muslim, but also a super human being with a terrific sense of humor to boot.

Now earlier, I talked about receiving belated bills, which had already been paid. I received another letter from the Mayo Clinic and opened it with my usual negative attitude towards receiving such communications. To my utter surprise, it was a refund check for a hundred odd dollars. The note said, that we had overpaid them.

Speaking of the Mayo Clinic, I received a most beautiful letter of sympathy from Dr. Karl Podratz, Chief of Gynecological Oncology at the clinic. I had sent him a letter informing him of what had happened and had enclosed my column that I wrote about you. Dr. Podratz said he read and reread my tribute and it reinforced his impressions of you when he first met you in 2002, and then in October of 2006, just six weeks before your passage.

I am trying to keep the house looking neat, but I am afraid it is a losing proposition. I don't know how you did it, to make the house look spotless and inviting. A few weeks ago, I had a weekend guest from Indiana. You probably never met Dr. Shaid Athar, but I have known him for many years through the Association of Pakistani Physicians of North America. He said our house is like an enchanting museum. Either he was being too polite or he needs a change of glasses because here and there you could see things that needed to be taken care of. But then, even the real museums have those spots, too.

Siraj and Munawar Ahmed are coming from Halifax, Nova Scotia, this weekend to spend a week with me. Monie is also coming for a few days. They will all attend The University of Toledo spring commencement where I am giving the commencement address on May 6, just nine days from now.

Do I need to say how much I miss you? Oh, how I wished you were here to help me with my commencement speech. You were my sounding board for such endeavors.

With all my love,
Amjad

APRIL 30, 2007

My Dearest Dottie,

The sun always rises after a dark, frightening night and the glorious spring always follows a dreary, cold winter. It has been a bit late, but finally the spring has arrived, not with a bang, but very gently and softly, tiptoeing into our hearts and our consciousness.

The trees are turning greener by the day—rather by the hour, if one could watch them closely. The white flowering trees in the front yard are about to bloom. Soon the flowering bushes by the swimming pool and by the fence will be alive with a collage of colors and a bouquet of fragrances. I have cleaned the patio furniture and placed cushions on them. In four weeks, we will have the opening of the pool and then we are going to dive head on into summer.

The new sliding doors in the pit and the one in the kitchen are just beautiful. On a slightly warm day I leave them open to bring in the cool and fresh air. It rejuvenates the house. The new bay window in the kitchen is also great!

The new doors and the new kitchen window need to be painted. Jim Emch, our trusted painter friend, has been waiting for the weather to change before he starts the paint job.

The kitchen is complete, as you had wanted it, but minus the floor. I decided to keep the old floor. I just didn't have the nerve, the heart or the patience to have that changed, too. Your new cupboards and black granite countertop look fabulous. The whole kitchen lights up in the late afternoon when the sun shines through the windows and illuminates the countertops. It was a good choice, Missy!

The carpets are also done. The Stanley Steamer crew did a great job. I have been living with some bad stains in the dining room, courtesy of well-meaning, but sloppy guests, back in December. The carpets are now spotless. The house should be presentable (perhaps a notch or two lower from your standards) to our guests this week.

I am in the middle of preparing my UT commencement address for its delivery. What do I say? Should I stand there in front of a crowd of eight to nine thousand and talk about lofty idealism and put everyone to sleep? It must be by now clear to you (I know it is) that I miss you in every facet of my life. Had you been around, you would have helped me refine my ideas and concepts.

You knew me so well and thus it would have been easy for you to match the message with the person delivering the message. Now how many long and boring commencement speeches we have sat/slept through?

Anyway, I have picked a theme: my experience as a Pakistani Muslim in America and my efforts through writings and other public discourses to pursue the path of integration without losing my ethnic or religious identity.

I have discussed my concept and have shared the broad outline of the address with Tasha, Qarie, and Monie, my current advisors. The three of them have unique perspective and they have shared their ideas, and in that light, I think I am going to have a good message.

I have decided to begin the address with an old story that I have narrated many times. A sixth-grade teacher assigned her students to write a short essay that would have to incorporate elements of religion, royalty, intrigue and suspense. One girl came out with the perfect example: Oh my God, the Queen is pregnant and I wonder who's done it? That one works every time.

Siraj and Munawar, as I said in my previous letter, are coming from Halifax for the occasion and will stay another week with me. Monie is flying in just for two days and will be leaving soon after the speech.

He has a dinner engagement in Florida that evening. I am inviting a handful of our friends to the commencement and to the subsequent lunch, which will be hosted by UT President Lloyd Jacobs for a small group of guests and the Board of Trustees.

Have I mentioned how much I miss you?
With all my love,
Amjad

MAY 6, 2007

My Dearest Dottie,

This morning I delivered my commencement address at The University of Toledo. I was told there were 8,000 people in attendance. You know I have been working on this address for months. In the process of putting my thoughts on paper, I missed my life-long critic-in-residence and your beaming, smiling, and nodding face in the audience. Our entire family was there with the exception of Qarie, who could not come from London. Monie came for two days and left soon after my speech to catch a flight to Florida. Tasha, Kevin and Hannah were there as were Pinchi, Siraj, Munawar, Naveed and Rehana, your sister Kim, her husband Tony, Razi and Shahida Rafeeq, Hussien and Randa Shousher, and Cherrefe Kadri. I dedicated my speech to you and Aapa, the two women who had such a big and positive influence on my life. I know for sure you would have been embarrassed to hear your name from the podium.

President Lloyd Jacobs, Dean Jeff Gold, and many other people were very complimentary. I am glad it is over.

The invitation to speak at the commencement took note of my non-medical interests. Specifically the university was interested in my role in Toledo as a writer and leader in the Islamic community.

You would be amused to hear the title of my talk: "The Empty Inkwells, The Queen's Bath and the Pursuit of Happiness: An American Journey." I discussed my experiences as a South Asian Muslim immigrant and my own pursuit of happiness, which is quite different than the happiness of having access to seventeen brands of toilet paper or long aisles of soft drinks in a grocery store. I guess my happiness came from the opportunity to think and write without any fear or intimidation.

Our kids are doing well. I think they have adjusted to your permanent absence from their lives. One evening, Monie and I had the opportunity to talk. He wondered how I was doing. I told him I was doing OK, but wondered how he was doing?

He manages to get by on a day-to-day basis, but sometimes he has a difficult time coping with your absence. Each time he is in Minneapolis to change planes, he breaks down and cries. It was from that airport that he always called you between flights. He would sit down with a cup of coffee and call you and the two of you would talk about happenings in our lives and his life. And while he was telling me all this, he cried. We both did. How could we not mourn the shared loss of someone we both loved so much? Will the intensity of loss ever diminish? When do the open wounds begin to heal? Is it always going to be so raw and fresh?

Every day I think of you a thousand times. Even outside the home the process continues. While driving down Manley Road, I think of you when passing Kazmaier's grocery store. I take shirts to Threadmill Cleaners, and I think of you. I pass Hannah's school, and I think of you. When buying groceries, I think of you. Your likes and dislikes were so intertwined with mine that each time I pick up an item in a store, I ask myself if you would approve. Instead of being jubilant that I don't have to seek your approval in everything I do, I still need your approval. I am not whole without you. A very significant part of me is missing and I can barely function without it.

I also thought of you the other day while listening to National Public Radio. You will be surprised to know that they are releasing *Dirty Dancing* in movie theaters across the country. It seems there are people who love the movie and wanted to see it on the big screen. I know how much you loved that movie. It was decidedly one of your most favorites, along with *A Few Good Men*.

I am enjoying the company of Siraj and Munawar. When I introduce Siraj to others and tell them that our friendship goes back fifty-three years, they don't believe it. He has been a very good friend and together, he and Munawar make a fine couple. He really loved you and cared for you, as I do for Munawar. They still regret that they didn't realize the gravity of your illness; otherwise they would have come to Toledo before leaving for Pakistan. Partly, it is my fault that I downplayed your illness to others, and partly your fault, because you did not want people to visit you when you were very sick.

Every night when turning off the bedside light, I do say good night to you. I miss putting my hand on your arm and drifting off to sleep.

Sleep well, my love.
Amjad

MAY 13, 2007

My Dearest Dottie,

Today was Mother's Day. It was a sad and melancholy day. Tasha called and asked if I would go with her and Hannah to visit you. I have been on the edge, so I was glad she called. We brought flowers with us and planted them on the grave. Hannah brought offering of peanut butter candy, your favorite. We stood there, in a light rain, holding each other and weeping. It is times like these, an anniversary or a holiday, that we feel how our lives have turned upside down. It is anyone's guess when we will get back to a semblance of normalcy.

I remember last year's Mother's Day. I had just returned from my visit to Pakistan and India. I had ordered a bouquet from Ken's Flower Shop, which pleased you a lot and we had dinner at Tasha's. Our Mother's Days were simple, but meaningful.

This morning while visiting you, I also took flowers from our yard. Perhaps some of the familiar fragrance would reach you and make you smile. There were lilacs that are now in full bloom in the garden. I also wanted to bring you a branch from the flowering trees in the front yard, but the wind and rain had done a number on them. They last less than two weeks in good weather, but wind and rain make them disappear much sooner. The brevity of their life makes them more beautiful and more appealing.

Siraj and Munawar left this evening for Canada. Before taking them to the airport, we stopped at the cemetery. It was my second visit today. I could imagine you smiling at seeing me twice in one day. One of these days, I am going to come with my blanket and writing pad and spend some time in your company. I promise not to bring my laptop. I don't want to irritate you. Lord knows how much you used to complain about me spending time on the computer. Strangely, I don't spend as much time with the computer now.

I am still trying to keep the house as you did, but I know I am falling short. A little bit of clutter is now part of my life and my home environment. I know you would not approve, but I am trying to strike a balance between your exact standards and my clutter-prone habits.

Two days ago, I hosted a dinner at our home in honor of Imran Ali and Noor Pirzada. They were recently promoted to the rank of professor in the department of neurology. I also invited a number of other people to come and celebrate their accomplishments. Rehana had volunteered to cook and she did, as usual, a wonderful job. (No, I didn't pressure her to do the cooking.) I invited Maseeh Rehman and his wife Tabinda, along with John Greenfield and his wife Holly. (John took care of you in December 2006 when you had that terrible paraneoplastic syndrome). All together there were close to twenty-five people. Tasha did a great job in preparing the house. Oh yes, Imran Adrabi and Rema also came along with Imran's father and his stepmother. Imran's father has liver cancer and has come from Pakistan for treatment. Siraj and Munawar enjoyed meeting some of the university people.

On the home front, I am having much difficulty finding stuff in the house. Remember our awkward accommodation? Whenever I asked you about something, you always got up, against my protestation, and got it for me. I would tell you a million times to just tell me where I could find it so I could get it myself. In this case, you acted just like your mother, whereas I—unlike your dad, Al Brown—was very willing to get it myself.

Well, guess what? I am having one hell of a time finding things. The other day, I had a visitor who wanted to see the old antique Gardenar china that we were given by the family in Peshawar, those red and blue teapots, bowls, and platters with the hand-painted designs. For the life of me, I could not find them. I looked for them in the glass cupboard in the living room where you displayed your Wedgwood collection, then in the china cabinet in the dining room, then in the pantry. Now I will have to go on a mission to find them. It is good that my life doesn't depend on some antique pottery made in a remote factory in Afghan hinterland in the early twentieth century.

On occasions, I will wander off to the storage room upstairs, our attic so to speak, and find long forgotten items that we collected over the period of forty years. Each one has a history and a story. Occasionally, I will bring one piece down and put it in a suitable place (my suitable has always been different than yours) and enjoy it.

Recently, I brought down the ceramic woman figurine we bought in Puerto Rico many, many years ago. She is the one with the colorful painted clothes, but no facial features. In her previous appearance, she sat there in the kitchen on the table in one corner for years. For a while she was on the back steps, and then she made her way upstairs to the great repository. Now she is back downstairs again. I am afraid without your balancing influence, the entire repository may find itself on the main floor. But I am still guided by your admonishments and your gentle nagging about these things. I will try to keep that in mind when I move things around. It reminds me the famous prayer of St. Augustine, "O Lord, give me chastity and continence ... but not yet."

Nasr Khan was here with his crew a few days ago and they did, as usual, a great job of sprucing up the bushes and shrubbery. He planted new flowers and spread mulch at the base of the trees and shrubs. It looks beautiful, just as you expected every spring.

I am trying hard to get into a routine or a semblance of a routine. But damn it, it is hard. I water plants when leaves start to wilt. I iron when I have a need of a shirt or a handkerchief. I am getting good at laundry but food is another story. Most evenings when I come home, I just warm up ready-made (heat & eat) Pakistani food. What a sad commentary from the times when we had our dinner in front of the TV, watching the news and talking. I still feel awkward going to a restaurant alone. Tasha would like me to come to her home for dinner every night, but I don't like doing that. But I do go there at least twice a week, if not more often.

I still feel your presence around me in the house. Every little noise or unexplained sound tells me you are here. The other night while reading in the living room, I heard a creaking on the floor upstairs. I called out loud for you to come down and talk to me, and I swore I wouldn't tell anyone. Only silence greeted what I thought was a rather generous offer.

Well, we must live in our own parallel universes, and until we find ways to communicate, I want you to know I love you very much.
Amjad

JUNE 2, 2007

My Dearest Dottie,

It has been two weeks since I wrote to you last. It is not that I have forgotten you. You are still on my mind constantly, and at times, more than constantly, if that is ever possible.

There have been more frequent episodes of restlessness and the gnawing feeling that my entire world is caving in. I know I am dealing with my grief in the best way I can, but I am not sure if there is something more significant lurking under the surface.
I kept thinking of my restlessness and the feeling of impending disaster and wondered if I was harboring some kind of self-destructive impulse. I was bothered with this to the point where I went to see a counselor. After a few sessions I was told that I am grieving and that there is no reason for concern. It did put my mind to rest somewhat.

Naveed and Rehana have been a great support. They drop in on occasions, and we talk about the kinds of things we used to talk about in the past. They are thinking of planning a vacation and would like me to join them. I have to think about it. For so many years the four of us vacationed together and enjoyed it immensely. There was our trip along the coastal highway in California, the Grand Canyon, Arizona, the Smoky Mountains and, of course, Maine. You had always wanted to go to Maine but somehow the few times when we were supposed to go, something would happen and we would cancel the trip. Once it was Naveed Farooki's untimely death in an auto accident. We finally did it in the summer of 2006.

It is amazing that despite a serious bout of paraneoplastic syndrome in December 2005—when I had all but given up hopes of your recovery—you bounced back. We not only did the Maine trip in June, but the Mexican trip with the Academy of Medicine in January 2006 and a family vacation to Los Angeles in April. In July, we had our annual picnic, and in October we went to Rochester, Minnesota for the consultation at the Mayo Clinic.

Excuse me, but I got a bit sidetracked. So, Naveed and Rehana would like me to join them on their next vacation. I told them to let me figure it out. Except for the fact that I am going to miss you very much, I don't see any other reason not to join them. We will see, as you used to say.

There are two anniversaries tomorrow. It will be six months since you left us. Let me rephrase: since we lost you. The former sounds as if you did it on purpose. It was something we all felt helpless about.

The other is Monie's thirty-third birthday. Oh, how well I remember the day in 1974, when soon after his birth, he developed complication after complication and had to be transferred from Lock Haven Hospital to Geisinger Medical Center in Pennsylvania. You came home on the third day of delivery, after a Caesarian section, and were deep in depression. When I came home after visiting Geisinger, you wondered if he was going to make it. We both wondered. And then you asked me to lay down with you and hold you close to me. It was one of the most tender and most comforting things we had ever done.

A shared grief was washed away, for a short time, by the proximity of two people who loved each other deeply.

Well, Monie is now thirty-three and has come of age. He is doing so well it scares me sometimes. To be able to manage a best selling-product for Allergan Inc.'s pharmaceuticals is indeed a great accomplishment. He called me a few days ago and told me that he is coming home for Father's Day. It will be great to see him.

Qarie is doing a play in London these days. It will end in early July, two weeks before my planned visit to England. I am going to attend the wedding of David Khwaja, the son of my friend Nasim. I hope to be able to see some friends during my visit. I must go and see Nisar Ahmed and his wife Bano in Birmingham. He was supposed to come to Peshawar last January, when I went after your passage, but he never showed up. I did give him a piece of my mind for standing me up. But he is such a dear friend, that I must set aside his occasional transgressions. Lord knows, my friends do that for me all the time.

I must close for now.

Rest in peace and remember you are always with me no matter where I am and what I am doing.
Amjad

My Dearest Dottie,

Summer is here, finally. The days are bright, somewhat humid, but cheerful and lovely. The lilacs are in full bloom. Nasr Khan has planted some beautiful flowers out front and the whole front of the house looks great. The days are long and protracted, as the sun sets after 9:30 p.m. and rises by 6 a.m. This is the kind of summer you loved so much. Tasha has brought hanging flower baskets and hung them by the front door and the kitchen window in the back of the house. The splashes of color go a long way to adding extra brightness and cheeriness to these sunny days.

The air conditioning is still off. I am going to hold out as long as I can. The nights are a bit uncomfortable, but a strategically placed fan does the job. The swimming pool is sparkly blue and inviting. Tasha's family has used it a few times already.

I have taken on the responsibility of watering the outdoor and indoor plants. Somehow, I get to do this chore late at night. The past two nights I watered them around midnight. The indoor plants also beg for attention and need watering at least a few times during the week. They all look very healthy. I am determined to keep your plants blooming. They remind me of you.

By the way, the ceramic life-size white cat on the patio lost her tail. I think the lawn-care people knocked her down. Now she sits in her frozen pose as if she wants to jump off the bench, but her upright tail is missing. Without that rudder, she is frozen stiff and even if she were to come alive, she would not be able to jump. She reminds me of Rehana's dog Rani when her tail had to be amputated after a car hit her. She looked so naked and weird without the fluffy cover over her rear. I had suggested to Rehana that she cover Rani's behind with a tiny diaper. Maybe I should do the same with the cat or better still, go buy a new one.

Ron Cowie came for a few days to photograph the commencement at Maumee Valley Country Day School. Tasha, Kevin, and young Kevin came over one evening to meet Ron, and we had supper on the patio. At such times, your grilled chicken is always on the menu. We call it Nano's chicken.

I am entering another phase of my life without you. At times I feel totally incapable of doing the most ordinary and mundane things. There is an ever-present sense under the surface that it is all a mirage, that we are all here for a short time. So what is the use? I have to resist that train of thought because I believe in living a good life with family, friends, music and the arts, etc. Your absence in the equation is dramatic and very distressing, but I need to keep moving. And I am.

One way to move on is to talk to people who are in the same situation as I. The underlying restlessness and simmering turmoil, which I talked about previously, have led me to talk to two counselors. Both suggested I am going through a normal grief process. The hospice counselor suggested I join a grief group of men who have lost their spouses. I joined the group and have attended three meetings so far. This is an interesting group. There are seven men ranging in age from fifty to over eighty. The sessions are coordinated by a minister and by a volunteer who lost his wife eight years ago.

I was struck by the similarity of our stories—not the details, but the essence of the stories. They all loved their spouses and are totally adrift without them. I was struck by the raw emotions each and everyone showed when asked to talk about their wives. It didn't seem to matter if they lost them a month ago or a year ago. They all broke down and cried, strapping strong men crying like babies. All I can say is that I liked sharing my feelings with them because, unlike anyone else, they really know how it feels to lose a part of your life, and a big part at that. There is only one session left, but I think the sessions may be extended by another two weeks.

I don't watch much television now. Even the evening *BBC World News* and the 6:30 p.m. network news are a hit or miss affair. But I did notice that your favorite actor Fred Thompson is making a run for Republican presidental nomination. If he is nominated and is (God forbid) elected president, he might take the cast of *CSI* to the White House. Then the reality and illusion will fuse and the West Wing will became a la-la land. Just imagine!

I mentioned earlier that the front of the house looks beautiful, with all the flowers that Nasir Khan and Tasha have planted. Just to keep up with our daughter (and whom am I kidding?), I power-washed the patio. It took me two days to finish the job but the patio looks good. I bought a big umbrella—a really big one—for the patio and also two outdoor fans. The propellers sit horizontally on top of lighted poles. They really look nice and elegant and have really jazzed up the otherwise Spartan patio. I need to have a few new things to look at, otherwise the view from the kitchen window would remain static and unchanging and that is depressing.

I had mentioned in one of my earlier letters that sometimes I have an overwhelming feeling of your presence in the house. Things happen that I can't explain. For example, one day last week, I looked for the newspaper that I had brought in. Later, Hannah found it in your Wedgewood display by the front door. I don't remember putting it there, but then I am a bit forgetful so maybe I did. Also last week, I was reading in the bedroom and I heard voices in the kitchen. It was morning and I thought Jim Emch had come to work in the kitchen. A little while later, I went to say hello to him and I realized that he and his crew had not yet arrived.

Was I imagining? Perhaps, but I am not sure. If you are here in some other ethereal dimension, then I must say you are a "friendly" ghost. I feel at peace when I am at home for I realize that while I may not be able to see you and talk to you, you are with me. If you could talk, you would be reminding me often about many things in the house that need my attention. When I power-washed the patio, I could not do it right, the way you would want it. Just the thought of that makes me smile.

I leave you with pleasant thoughts of our life together and wish you peace.

As always, your
Amjad

JUNE 18, 2007

My Dearest Dottie,

Today was Father's Day. Monie came from California for two days to be with me on this occasion. I tried to tell him that it was not necessary, but he thought it was important that he come.

It was a busy weekend. Friday I had a dinner for Sue Ott Rowlands, the outgoing dean of arts and sciences at The University of Toledo. She is the one who helped in the final push for the Khattab Chair in Islamic Studies. Monie arrived that afternoon and joined us. Tasha made dinner, and it was wonderful having thirty people enjoying themselves on the patio. Tammie, the woman who helps serve and wash the dishes, was not available, so Tasha asked Hannah and two of her friends to fill in. They were great. They served appetizers, did the dishes and cleaned up. We paid them the money we would have paid the wait staff. Everything went like a charm.

The next day, Saturday, Monie joined Tasha and me to attend Penny Reed's wedding. It was a small wedding (about eighty people) and was very tastefully done. She and her husband Garry Moran looked extremely happy. Penny whispered to me that you were there in spirit. Perhaps she was right, but I would have liked you to be sitting next to me instead.

Today was a low-key affair. We had a leisurely lunch on the patio before Monie left for the airport. Although he was here for just two days, it meant so much to Tasha, Kevin, and me.

Qarie is doing a play in London these days, *Get Away* by Greg MacArthur, and he has a lead role. He sent us a recent review and it was extremely complimentary. I can't wait for him to come home in six weeks. Tasha was thinking of having a small party for him to mark his American debut at the Purple Rose Theatre. She is talking about a small party, but somehow her definition and my definition of "small" is just not the same. I bet by the time it is done, we will have had close to 100 people.

Your definition of small was always correct. It was me who had difficulty with it. Remember our wedding, when we both agreed that we would have a small one? When I handed you the list of my guests, you were taken aback. That list was close to 200 people. You asked innocently, "I thought we had decided to have a small wedding." But for me, having 300 guests was a small affair. Back home it would have been a very small wedding indeed. I think we ended up with close to 400 guests. But as we matured and understood each other, you did make allowances for my definition of small. I think when it comes to such definitions, our daughter has a dominant Y chromosome.

We have encountered some problems with the cemetery people. They don't allow any flowers on the grave. The flowers must be in a retractable vase built into the marker. Your granite marker doesn't have a vase. They may not be prompt in the upkeep of the cemetery, but they sure are very prompt in removing bouquets of flowers left on the grave.

Then we had a problem ordering a bench, to which the cemetery had agreed. They say we can't have a bench so close to a nearby bench. The distance between the two benches has to be forty feet. The lady I am dealing with is a most difficult and obstinate person. She would not give me the name and phone number of her supervisor. I did track down someone in Cincinnati and talked to him. First, he gave me the runaround about the rules they have to enforce. Their rules keep proliferating like the summer weeds, and they feel no obligation to keep the promise they made to me.

As I was not getting anywhere with them, I told them that I will relocate your remains to another Toledo cemetery. That scared the hell out of them. Just imagine if such news hit the press. Now the bench can be placed where we want and should be here in a month.

I swear the whole funeral and cemetery industry is a big racket. The cemetery owners also own a company that makes grave markers and benches. All benches have to be granite, with the cheapest about $1,800. Why can't one have a comfortable park bench rather than a cold granite slab to sit on? They say they have rules to follow except they make the rules and then expect everyone to fall in line. Shame on them.

I am using the patio and the deck more and more. Last week I had a poetry recital on the deck by the pool. You remember Dr. Munib Rahman, the retired professor of modern languages, who lives in Ann Arbor? I mentioned in one of my earlier letters that his Swiss wife of fifty years died two years ago. It was a memorable evening. Later we served green tea and sweets.

My evenings are still empty and boring. I am getting lazy when it comes to food. I eat, but not appropriately. I again sit in the front of the TV with whatever I can find in the refrigerator and watch the news and follow it with two of our favorites, *Wheel of Fortune* and *Jeopardy*.

Occasionally I am startled to hear your name on TV: "*The BBC News Hour* was made possible through a grant from S. Amjad and Dorothy G. Hussain Family Fund." You always looked so embarrassed when you heard and saw that announcement.

You did well, Dottie Ji, and I loved you with all my heart and soul. I still do.

Yours as always,
Amjad

ORLANDO, FLORIDA

JULY 2, 2007

My Dearest Dottie,

It is that time of the year again, when the Association of Physicians of Pakistani Descent of North America holds its summer meeting. The meeting is in Orlando this year. Tasha, Kevin, Hannah, and Kevin II (as I'll call him now) came to join me for the weekend.

The APPNA meeting was the biggest ever and was well-organized. Slight glitches always happen, but considering the size of the meeting those small irritants were not that important.

I had rented a two-bedroom suite, which worked out great. We enjoyed the sitting area, had our meals there and enjoyed the large parlor.

The Khyber Medical College Alumni dinner was special this year. Unbeknownst to me, the president had asked Omar Atiq to pay a tribute to you, which he did in the most eloquent way. He shared a few stories with the group. I was a bit uncomfortable, for the alumni had never done such a thing before. But they wanted to acknowledge your contributions to the Khyber Alumni. In my remarks that followed, I thanked them for their gesture and then said we have already had too much gloom. We should change our focus and enjoy the evening. I told some funny stories about the college and some of the alumni to set the mood, and soon we were all laughing. You would have liked it.

I also took Dr. Zahid Khalil with me to the meeting. He is a professor of forensic medicine at Khyber Medical College and is spending three months in the Pathology Department at The University of Toledo Medical Center. He is working with Dr. James Patrick in the Lucas County coroner's office. Dr. Khalil is the eighth visiting professor to have come to UTMC in Toledo under the program that you and I started ten years ago. The push for increasing the endowment that we undertook last year was successful. We added $50,000 to the $150,000; it now stands at $200,000. I have asked the alumni to help bring it up to $250,000.

The banquet Saturday night, two days ago, was also great. Tasha accompanied me to the banquet, and this time, unlike the New York meeting a few years ago when she had joined me, everybody treated her with the utmost love and affection. In that New York meeting, the two of us sat with strangers who thought I was her sugar daddy.

I met many people at APPNA who did not know of your passing. It was awkward for them to offer condolences in the midst of the festivities. But they genuinely felt your absence. A few gave me checks for the visiting lectureship that has been established in the College of Nursing. I also saw the celebrated poet Ahmad Faraz at the meeting. He is the one who had stayed with us a number of years ago and left us a poem, which he wrote on the invitation card we'd made for his recital. He also felt bad for not knowing about your passing.

Anyway, this is something I have been dealing with for the past seven months. Not a single week goes by that I do not come across someone who had not heard of your passage. God knows how long it will go on. I only say this because on occasions, the person is beside himself or herself, and I end up consoling them. Many people don't know how to react. They swear they had not heard and I have no reason (or right) not to believe them.

In two weeks, I am going to England and am looking forward to the trip. I think it will be good for Qarie and me to spend some time together. Qarie is happy when he is working and happy to be on stage in London.

On the way back from Orlando, I saw Monie at the Detroit airport. He was between flights and had coordinated his Detroit arrival with my itinerary. We had only twenty minutes but it was so good to see him. I tell you, had it not been for our kids, I don't know how I would have coped with your passing. Monie told me he is coming home for a weekend in two weeks. All I can say is what you were so fond of saying about our kids—"They are something." Something indeed.

Rest in peace my love. I love you so much, and I miss you so much.
Amjad

JULY 4, 2007

My Dearest Dottie,

It is past midnight on the Fourth of July. Tasha, Kevin, and Kevin II were here this evening for a cookout. Tasha brought food, and we had a wonderful quiet dinner (as quiet as it can be with a hyperactive two-year-old) on the patio. We swam and relaxed. I hung the flag on the front porch this morning. I like to see Old Glory fluttering in the breeze.

After Tasha and Kevin left, I busied myself in preparing wedding poems for the forthcoming weddings in the community. Abida and Wakil Khan's daughter Warda is getting married on August 4. Nawaz and Bajo Chaudhary's daughter Tina (Rashada) will be married a week later. It seems I have been, of late, doing a lot of calligraphy. A few days ago, I finished one for Nasim Khawaja's son who will be married in London in six weeks. It is lot of work, but I believe a framed poem in Urdu calligraphy makes a great wedding gift. These girls are rather dear to me, and I can't think of a more symbolic or appropriate gift. It is tedious and time consuming, but it sure beats a set of linen or china.

Nawaz Chaudhary also sprung a surprise. He wants me to perform his daughter's wedding. Imam Farooq is on vacation for two months and in his absence, some of us are called upon to perform such duties. It is good that in Islam, every Muslim can perform duties that are traditionally assigned (or consigned) to an imam. This will be the fifth or sixth wedding I will perform.

After a spouse's passing, many people have all kinds of regrets. I have been having some regrets also. I regret that I didn't help you out more in the household chores. I realize now how difficult it is to keep the house tidy and presentable: to clean the house, do the laundry, cook meals, water the plants, pay bills, fulfill social obligations and what not. I marvel how you juggled everything by yourself. My contribution was—at the most—sweeping the patio occasionally, tidying up the study and putting out the garbage on Sunday evenings.

This morning I was in the mood for breakfast. Since you left, I haven't had a sit-down breakfast by myself. It is just too painful to re-enact the ritual by myself. In the last year or so, you reluctantly let me fix breakfast for us. Actually, I became rather proficient at fixing vegetable omelets and simple fried eggs.

So I set the table for two in the dining room with good china and sparkling silverware. I fixed fried eggs and toast and cut-up fruit. I brought everything, including butter and my favorite orange marmalade, to the table. I sat in my favorite chair and enjoyed the breakfast. Your plate remained clean, but it didn't matter. While eating I carried on a conversation as if you were sitting and listening. It felt good. Both my stomach and my mind felt happy.

A few days ago while surfing television channels, I stumbled upon the *Montel Williams Show*. A woman by the name of Sylvia Browne was his guest. She is a psychic and seemed to know the answer to every question the audience asked. It was great showmanship, where the psychic—the appellation "psychologist" would be more fitting—knew the vulnerability of the audience. The audience was mostly women and she answered their inquiries in an emphatic and reassuring way. For example:

> Q: My husband died three years ago. I knew he wanted to say something before he died, but we couldn't understand what he was trying to say?
>
> A: Honey, he was trying to tell you he loved you.
>
> Q: Is my husband at peace?
>
> A: Yes, he is and still loves you.

And so on ...

Now I was waiting for an answer like this:

"He is burning in hell and regrets being so mean to you" or "He is still in purgatory and it will be a long time before he moves out of there. He is happy, but not very." Or, "He is very happy and content because he no longer has to put up with your nonstop nagging."

This life-after-death concept is unique and fascinating. If hope springs eternal, then the hope to see loved ones again does help reduce the acute pain of permanent separation.

You have always believed in life after death, but over the years I have lost my emphatic belief in the concept. Now wouldn't it be surprising if I keel over and find myself being welcomed by you and others in another world? You will forgive me if my first question is, "Honey, what is for dinner?" I do miss your cooking, the aroma of basmati rice, and sizzling *chapli kabobs*.

Ghalib, my favorite 19th century Urdu poet, had said it aptly:

> *Hum ko maaloom hai janat ki haqiqat laikan*
> *Dil ke khush rakhne ko Ghalib yeh khial acha hai*

"I know the reality of heaven. It is a great idea to keep one happy and pacified."

Nothing much is going on here. Monie will be home for the weekend in few days. I am leaving soon afterwards for London for ten days to see Qarie and attend the wedding of David Khwaja, my friends Nasim and Chris's son. I will also make the obligatory visit to Birmingham to see Nisar. I also intend to stay a day or so with Pauline and Tony Shelbourne, the wonderful English couple from Swanton. They moved back to the UK after Tony's retirement from Dana Corporation. It will be fun to visit them. They are so gracious.

That is all for now.
Yours as always,
Amjad

JULY 17, 2007

My Dearest Dottie,

I had been thinking of writing an essay about my frame of mind at this juncture, seven months after you left. With each passing day, the urge to write such a piece became stronger. After being in the support group for seven weeks, I have had ample opportunities to assess my situation and compare it with those of others.

I wrote the essay and two days ago, it was published as my *Blade* column. The response has been nothing short of amazing. I had written that while I look OK and apparently am doing well, there is still a raging storm inside me. Sometimes the storm eases off but at times, it is unbearable.

I also mentioned the awkward and clumsy ways some friends and acquaintances express their condolences. Some are amusing, but others have been outright insulting.

Most of the people who wrote are themselves in the same state as I am. Some are dealing with it years after the death of their spouses and, in some cases, decades. One wonders if the crushing weight of loss ever gets lighter or goes away completely. I hope so. Life would be impossible if there is no healing.

I heard from many people you had known: Diana French, Jeri Milstead, Ann Baker, and tens of others. People I had not heard from in twenty years wrote and, of course, also from total strangers. The common refrain was, "I identify with the feeling." I heard from a lady who runs the gift shop at Bay Park Hospital. She said she used to see you come in the shop every Tuesday and Friday (your chemotherapy days) to look around and buy candles. She often wondered (as did her coworkers) who you were. One time, you didn't have cash to pay for the purchase, so you wrote a personal check. After you left, she immediately phoned her coworker to tell her who you were. She talked about your gentleness, your grace and your kindness towards her and others. She was compelled to write when she read the column.

My laments aside, I do feel a measure of peace coming to my mind. I am starting to take a longer view of life, or at least trying to. I realize I have to make progress toward the normalcy of every day of life. It ain't easy! When I see happy couples, I feel a deep pain in my heart for a way of life that was once but is no more.

It is strange how two people living together adjust to each other. I don't think God has created carbon copies of his creations. We are different, but over time, we learn to smooth the annoying and grating rough edges. I was very sensitive to your needs, tip-toeing around the bedroom when I got up in the morning. You always told me it was not necessary, but since you were a light sleeper, I couldn't impose my early morning awakening on you. Similarly, while staying in hotels, I would go to the bathroom and read there, sitting on the floor until you awoke. You protested (to the point of being angry), but I had to do it. Since I was doing that out of love, you started to accept it, but it took you a long time. We did compromise, however, and I would place the bedside lamp on the floor, covering it with two towels. That took the glare away but still gave me enough light to read and write.

The other day I was going over my finances with Tasha. The household expenses have remained rather constant. The food bill is drastically down, but food had always been a relatively inexpensive item on the long list of our expenses. Sometimes, I entertain the idea of downsizing, but then both you and I were traditionalists. We enjoyed living in this big house, enjoyed the kids coming home and sleeping in their own rooms, and welcoming guests without crowding anyone. The cost is steep, but at least for the moment, it is well worth the price tag. You had always told me that if I had my way, I would have guests staying with us all the time. Your penchant for privacy and your high standards of entertaining did put a damper on my urge to invite people at the drop of the hat. And still we had hundreds of people come through our home over the years.

Isn't it wonderful not to have financial worries? But then we never had financial problems. From a surgery resident's salary of a few $100 a month in the 1960s to 750 rupees a month in Peshawar ($75, the amount made by an assistant professor at that time), to a whopping $50,000 in Lock Haven, Pennsylvania in the early 1970s—quite a swing. But did we (particularly you) ever complain? We made do with whatever we had, and had a good time doing it.

Oh, how vividly I remember our three years in Peshawar. Seven hundred and fifty rupees didn't stretch that far, and we always had a lot of month left at the end of the money. I think about the one pound of chocolate ice cream I brought home once a month on payday. It was the best ice cream we have ever had before or since. Or how about the time when Aapa cooked a chicken for some guests and Tasha, age three, went wild seeing the chicken on the table? In those days we mostly ate beef (the cheapest cut) and vegetables. Chicken, lamb, and fish were for special occasions and special friends. These ruminations remind me of Charles Lamb's famous essay, "Old China."

I am getting ready and getting excited to go to England. I leave in the next two days. Just remember you are always with me wherever I am, and you are always in my thoughts.

With all my love,
Amjad

EN ROUTE FROM LONDON TO DETROIT
JULY 28, 2007

My Dearest Dottie,

I am returning home after a rather busy ten-day stay in England. Qarie is doing well and he looks good. It was such a joy to see him and spend some time with him. Qarie went back to London in April after having been home for almost four months, and was feeling down for a while after his return. As you know, he is the one who needs people around him. He spent a few weeks with his friends, the Bantings, and house-sat for them. A job on stage came along and he reluctantly accepted it. His heart was not in it for he was still mourning.

During the play's two-month run, he immersed himself in it, setting aside his grief and his pain. But the pain doesn't go away; it is merely postponed. So after the play ended, he found himself overwhelmed by dark clouds of despair. Tasha and Monie phoned him a lot and helped him climb out of the abyss. My trip came just in time, and we had ample time to talk. It is amazing how just the presence of a dear one lifts one's spirits. We both felt that way. We talked on the trains, at home and in pubs and restaurants. It was very soothing and therapeutic. He talked at length about how you and he spent time in the garage, both of you having retreated for a smoke. He would play guitar and the two of you would talk for hours.

He is looking forward to coming home in a month to do the play in Chelsea. And it will be so good to have him home. But he doesn't want to come back to an empty house—I will be in California visiting Monie when he arrives from London. So he will now fly from London to New York, go to Rhode Island to see his best friend Ron Cowie, and then they will drive to Toledo in time for my return.

I spent two days with Tony Shelbourne at his cottage in the Cotswolds region of England. It is an hour and a half train ride from London. Pauline was in the U.S., visiting their daughter who lives in Waterville near Toledo. The Shelbournes live in a beautiful cottage in the village of Minety where they raise sheep on four idyllic acres. Their garden is beautiful, much more so than the one they had near Toledo. Tony was a perfect host, and I really enjoyed myself.

He took me around the village to meet people in the small convenience store (the only business in the village), to pubs, and to an Indian restaurant in a nearby village. The food was excellent, but the manager and waiters were rude and insulting. I also witnessed the deluge from torrential rains that fell relentlessly for an entire day and night, dumping close to eight inches of water and causing the rivers to swell and overflow their banks. We were marooned in the village for about four hours and had to find a circuitous route back to his cottage. We were ready to park the car, wade through two and a half feet of water, and walk home, barely one and a half miles from where we were stranded. I thought it would have been a great adventure but we were spared the excitement.

David Khawaja's wedding was an elegant affair held in the Ramada Edwardian Hotel near Heathrow Airport. We had stayed there with our kids on a few occasions on our way to and from Pakistan. I had prepared a *Sehra* in calligraphy, and had it framed. Somehow the large frame survived the trans-Atlantic travel and was prominently displayed on an easel during the reception. I also took a printed poem, with the translation, and they were placed at each place setting. Qarie read the English translation and I read the original Urdu. Needless to say, Nasim and his extended family were very pleased.

Shafqat and Katherine Hussain were there as well. After the reception, I went with them to stay at their home. She is such a gracious lady. We talked about you and about the last time you and I stayed with them. I slept in the same room where we were then. It brought back a torrent of memories. What a comfortable and inviting home they have. Shafqat, Nasim, and Arshad Javed have been so kind all these past months. They have called so many times to make sure I am doing OK.

Arshad Javed and his wife Saadia were at the wedding as well. I did some sightseeing with them, and they took me to Solihull to Nisar Ahmed and Bano's home. I'd stayed with them the last two days of my last England visit. It was so good to see them. Nisar is a man of few words, as you know, but we click. Our friendship spans almost fifty years and Nisar has not changed an iota so far as that friendship is concerned. We called Fazle Akram in London and he also joined us. We had a great time talking into the wee hours of the morning. You were very much a part of our talks. Nisar's relationship with you (as with Siraj, Alaf Khan, Naveed, and Saeed) was very special. They all loved you so much and during our conversations, you were mentioned often and with lots of love.

Nisar fondly recalled that you called him Nisar Masih, meaning Nisar the Christian. You never forgot when he, in his funny mood, had announced to the staff of the Mission Hospital in Peshawar (where he and I worked as surgeons) that for the next month, the month of Ramadan, he would be Nisar Masih and not Nisar Ahmed. It was so damn funny, it stuck; you used to call him Nisar Masih much to his amusement.

Fazle Akram, our friend from London, amazes me. He underwent a radical prostatectomy for cancer about two years ago and had a recurrence for which he underwent radiation therapy. If you look at him, you wouldn't know he has had health problems. More than his physical wellbeing, he has a very positive attitude and takes such adversities in stride. Who else would be able to do that, when afflicted with cancer and having an ill wife and an ill daughter?

As I fly back home (in another two hours I will be in Detroit), I look
forward to getting into my familiar and soothing environment.
I know it is going to be difficult for a day or two, but I have been
through this before and I think I can cope. After I get home, I am
coming to visit you. It calms me down when I visit you, even though
our conversations are now one-sided.

During all the years we have been married, we had a code word for
"I love you." If there were other people around, we both were used to
say, "You know what?" the answer was never communicated but was
always, "I love you."

You know what?
Amjad

EN ROUTE, NEWPORT BEACH, CALIF.,
TO WASHINGTON, D.C.

AUGUST 26, 2007

My Dearest Dottie,

The past week has been a whirlwind. Last week, Ohio Gov. Ted
Strickland announced my long-anticipated appointment to The
University of Toledo Board of Trustees. It was an "iffy" appointment
until the last moment. The only concern was that I write an opinion
column for *The Blade*. They just didn't want an opinion columnist
on the board, because he might write unfavorable things about the
university and or the state government. I assured them that as a
trustee, I consider writing about the university inappropriate and thus
will hold myself to my own ethical and moral standards. I will not
write about the university or higher education in the state.

There were people in Toledo who approached me and tried to talk me into giving up my column. I politely refused. How could I give up the opportunity and the privilege to address pressing issues of religion and inter-religious amity in our town? John Block has supported my appointment whole-heartedly and never asked me to entertain the possibility of not continuing to write my column. In a conversation I had with John Haseley, the governor's chief of staff, I declined to accept the conditions and said I would rather not be appointed to the board. Apparently, they got the point and relented.

The Blade carried the story the next day and followed a few days later with an editorial. And to top it off (how embarrassing you would say), in today's paper, they did a Sunday front-page profile of me. I am really embarrassed by all this hoopla. I wish John Block had not requested the profile, but he thinks this appointment breaks the old mold of only business people or politicians being appointed to university boards. I am so embarrassed to face the Board of Trustees because, by propping me up, the article inadvertently cast a negative light on other board members. I think all of them are extremely competent, and they bring much expertise and know-how to the table.

While all this was happening, I left town for Newport Beach, Calif., to spend a long weekend with Monie. We had the most pleasant time together. We had lunch with some of his coworkers (a pleasant and very likeable bunch), played squash (he beat me) and spent an afternoon at the beach, which is a few minutes walk from his apartment. We sat on beach chairs and talked about you and how much we miss you, about his life, his future plans, and a lot more. He wants to get married, but he wants a woman who will be sensitive to his religious and cultural needs. Our little boy has grown up to be a fine young man.

One evening, Calvin McEllwine, Amy Adray, and Noor Ahmed came, and we had an enjoyable evening at a Pakistani restaurant.

Now, I am on my way to Pinehurst, N.C., to visit my friend Mohsin Ali and his wife Dolores. Mohsin, as you know, is the retired diplomatic editor from Reuters, London. Upon his retirement, he was decorated by Queen Elizabeth with an Order of the British Empire [OBE] award. He has been a mentor and helped me tremendously in my column writing. I call him a guru, which in Hindi and Urdu means a respected teacher.

Our annual picnic is on but almost two months late. It is going to be on September 8. We had a family discussion, and everyone thought we should continue the tradition. (We are also having Thanksgiving.) The good thing is that both Qarie and Monie will be here. It will be the same familiar site—the tent, ice cream, delicious food and friends. The only difference will be you won't be here.

Did I tell you I miss you very much?
Yours as always,
Amjad

SEPTEMBER 12, 2007

My Dearest Dottie,

A lot has happened since I wrote to you last. The biggest thing was our annual picnic. While we had made the decision to carry out the tradition—because you would have wanted us to—we did not realize how time consuming and taxing it would be. We divided the chores, and our daughter took on what you used to do and much more. Mind you, we were rather late for this year's picnic. In other years, it was held in July or early August. This year it was in September.

Because of a forecast for rain, we got a bigger main tent and had a smaller one connecting the big tent with a passage to the garage. Then, just to make sure, we had a third tent over the patio by the kitchen. Arbid Wehabi from the Grape Leaf Restaurant catered the food and, as usual, he was terrific and very accommodating. Three hundred people turned up. It was festive but there was also a lingering sadness because of your absence. Many of our guests thought they felt your presence; many others intentionally looked for you or at least expected you to appear from the side of the house. You were in everyone's thoughts and were deeply missed.

I remember last year, despite your being ill and not feeling well, you made it a point to greet every guest and talk to each one. You would go into the house and rest for fifteen to twenty minutes before coming out and spending another hour or so with the guests. You did that many times during the course of the afternoon. You were amazing!

The ice cream truck was, as usual, the big hit, even with the adults. I guess ice cream unites adults and children on the same happy-childhood level. Not only did they enjoy ice cream to their hearts' desire, on the way out, some took more ice cream home with them. They wouldn't do that with the other food, would they? Well, as I said, ice cream does make some adults act like children.

The rain held off until late in the evening when the party was over and the guests had left. Some of us—Naveed, Rehana, Elaine and her family from Columbus (Qarie's theater professor), Bruce and Rebecca, Tasha and her family, and and our two boys—sat under the patio tent and enjoyed each other's company. Oh, I forgot Ruth Black, Tasha's mother-in-law, was there, too. She had come a week earlier and stayed for the picnic, while and Monie was with us for two days. We sat there for hours, enjoying the music and the rain. It was just beautiful to sit under the tent and have the rain all around us.

Your friends at A to Z Rentals were great. You probably know that Joyce, the matriarch of the A to Z clan, has passed away. I was traveling when she made her passage and was not able to go to the funeral. Tasha attended the service on our behalf. Joyce was a wonderful lady, and you two had connected in some very special way. It was so kind and considerate of her to have visited you just days before your departure. It was hard for her to drive because of her back and hip problem, but she did. And then she came to the funeral home as well. How considerate!

Qarie has started his rehearsals in Chelsea, commuting from home to Michigan. The Purple Rose Theater Company has given him a furnished house in Chelsea, which he intends to use when he is there late in the evening or when he has matinees. We are all planning to see the play and spend the night at his new accommodation. The play is *The Poetry of Pizza* by Deborah Breevort, and your son has a lead role.

The house looks OK despite Qarie's being here. He gets sloppy at times, as he is prone to, but overall he manages to keep his immediate vicinity tidy and clean.

Your memorial lecture is coming up in three and a half weeks. The College of Nursing has invited Melodie Chenevert, a nationally known nurse, to give two presentations on October 11 at the UT Health Science Campus. We are looking forward to it.

Ramadan starts tomorrow. I am going to miss you a whole lot more during this month. I will miss our simple evening meal, after breaking the fast with dates and fruit chat. I am getting used to so many other things, and I am sure I will somehow plough through this period as well. People have started inviting me for *iftar* dinners but so far, I have declined them all. I would rather be home, even if alone, than be surrounded by chattering and gossiping crowds during this very special period of penance.

Peace and blessing!
Amjad

SEPTEMBER 18, 2007

My Dearest Dottie,

Today is your birthday. You would have been sixty-three years old today, had the cruel hand of death not snatched you from me. Though we were not into celebrating birthdays with fanfare, we did observe them, usually with a quiet dinner, more often than not at home, a bouquet of flowers and a genuine wish for happiness.

Anniversaries and special days are rather difficult for me. I am, on such days, always torn apart between what used to be and what is now. That distance is short — nine months in our case — but I have the feeling I am traveling on a dark and lonely road. Sure, there are bright patches along the way, but the feeling of utter helplessness and profound despair is always lurking in the shadows. Each time I see a light at the end of a tunnel, it is somehow followed by another long tunnel.

Last Sunday, I visited the cemetery to spend some time with you. I keep my favorite coarse Peshawari blanket in the car now. I spread the blanket by you and lay down in the warm sun. It was soothing and comforting. You were six feet down in another subterranean world, and I was on the surface trying to understand the distance measured in eons.

Today, your birthday, I took you some roses, laid them on the marker and wished you a happy birthday. And suddenly, I was struck by the absurdity of it all. As I said earlier, we never celebrated birthdays with any fanfare, but we did have private moments with quiet dinners and conversation about our life together. I tried to do that while visiting you, but my emotions got the best of me and I sat there shedding tears of despair.

Tasha was also in a melancholy mood today. We had dinner at her place. It is Ramadan and breaking of the fast is around 7:15 p.m. It was a quiet, pensive, but satisfying dinner. She is such a lady! I can't tell you how proud I am of her.

Happy birthday, my love. You would have been sixty-three years old today. Though the clock stopped nine months ago, in my mind it is still ticking.

Amjad

OCTOBER 6, 2007

Dearest Dottie,

It has been more than three weeks since I wrote last. I do talk to you all the time but haven't had the peace of mind or a tranquil moment to sit down and write. No, I am not working myself ragged. I am not any busier than I have been since my retirement four years ago. Or was it five years? I lose track of time easily.

For the past many weeks, I have been rather preoccupied with the idea of my death. Not that anything is imminent. I am doing well, but there is a deep down feeling that perhaps my time is up. You remember a few years ago, when I had the same feeling and I talked to you. You got a bit testy and said, "If you keep thinking about it, it will happen." I don't know why, but at that time the number sixty-seven had stuck in my mind. I thought I was going to die at sixty-seven. There was no rhyme or reason to that number. It just got stuck in my mind. But I survived that milestone. If my premonition had come true, I would have left a full one year ahead of you. I am glad it didn't happen. I take a measure of satisfaction in the fact that I was able to take care of you during your illness, particularly the last months of your life.

110

This prediction of death is a funny business. In history, some people have accurately predicted the time or manner of their death. A poet and writer living in Delhi during the nineteenth century had a premonition that he would die of injuries from a fall. He even predicted the date. And it all came true.

You remember that Arabic, Persian, and Urdu all share most of the same alphabet. And each letter is given a corresponding number. The beauty is to come up with a phrase or a sentence either by itself or within a poem, that when broken into its individual letters and the assigned numbers, will provide a date or year. The Delhi poet said, *Dast o bazoo bashikast*/A broken hand and arm. And indeed, he fell from his roof, sustained a broken hand and arm. When numbers from these letters were added together, the total was the year of his death.

In my case, I kept thinking of a Persian phrase that seemed to be stuck in my mind. Literally translated it says, "The story ended with a broken heart." A tally of numbers came to 2005, but it was a false alarm. Lucky for me.

Meanwhile, my membership on the Board of Trustees has been going well. I was initially overwhelmed with all the meetings and material I was being sent. It is still going on, but I am handling it a bit more efficiently. It is almost a full time job with no compensation. I hope I will be able to contribute somewhat. There is so much to learn. There are some very decent and well-informed people on the Board, and I will learn so much from them.

Qarie has been staying in Chelsea most of the week for his play. They started full dress rehearsals in front of an audience last week. Tasha, Hannah, and Kevin went to one rehersal and they came back impressed. I will go with Monie this week. Our son is the star of the show and he is enjoying it. It would have made you so proud. Good thing he is going to be around for another three months.

Last week, I was in the mood to clean the refrigerator. A few things had spilled and made the glass shelves sticky. I discarded whatever food I had to and gave the shelves and drawers a good scrubbing. It was hard, for I had never done it, but it was very enjoyable and satisfying. After I finished, I mopped the kitchen floor—another first. I did it with some trial and error (lots of error). But I got the tiles sparkling.

As I was doing these chores that you always called mindless, I was struck with an irony. All these years as you struggled to keep the house, appliances, floors and furniture clean and sparkling, I never offered a word of appreciation. I assumed that all this cleaning just happens.

After I did the floor and refrigerator, I wanted someone to take a look and appreciate my work. When Tasha came to visit, I had her look inside the refrigerator, and she was impressed. At least she said she was. Can I still ask you to forgive me now for being so unappreciative? Oh, how do we get stuck in our individual grooves?

Ramadan is going well. Only four more days left. It is usually at sunset, when I break my fast, that I miss your presence. You always prepared the simple evening meal with so much love and care … the dates and cut-up fruit with a cup of coffee to break the fast before evening prayers and then the meal. I do all that, but some of the spiritual dimension you added to my fasting is missing. Tasha knows how special this month is for me and how you took care of me. She comes quite often, bringing food with all the trimmings. Other times, I go over to her home and break the fast. She does everything the way you did. It makes me so very proud of her.

You remember we had planned to have a special *iftar* dinner during Ramadan for a limited number of people. We thought we would invite a Jewish and Christian couple, our friends Naveed and Rehana, and also Tasha and Kevin. Having these special people around the table at a very special time of the year, meant we could enjoy each other's company, share our traditions and learn from one another as well. That didn't happen, and I don't think I will be able to have it this year. Perhaps next year.

I must close for now. It is close to *iftar* time and I am going to have my simple little dinner and think of you, as I sit in front of the TV watching *Jeopardy*.

With all my love,
Amjad

ANGOLA, INDIANA
OCTOBER 21, 2007

My Dearest Dottie,

I am in Angola, Indiana, at Munir's cottage for our biannual card group outing. I am glad the group decided to come here instead of going to our cottage. Even though we had a good time at our place, I still get lonely when I am there. We both made it the way we wanted it; the cottage, in my mind, was always associated with you. While I am getting a lot more comfortable living alone in our home in Maumee, I don't have that peace of mind when I go to the cottage. But perhaps it will get better in due course.

On the way here I stopped at the cottage to make sure everything was OK. It was. The place looked neat, clean, and very inviting. The most enjoyable part of my brief stop was driving through the forest on the long (isn't it half a mile?) driveway. It was late afternoon and in the light of the setting sun, the whole forest was ablaze with red, yellow, orange, green, brown, and crimson colors. I have not seen such beautiful and vivid fall colors in many years. This inspired me to write a cover story for *Toledo Medicine* on autumn. It is a photo essay and is scheduled to come out in about a month.

The dynamics of our card group have not changed much. We all have our peculiar idiosyncrasies and our quirks, but we get along fine. People are always surprised that seven odd people spending a weekend together could have so much fun. Everyone brought his assigned food and as always, we had more, much more, food than needed. My assignment was to bring breakfast items. Since your departure, I am now being asked to bring groceries, etc., and not cooked food. They are wise—knowing my total inability (and ineptness) to cook anything. We had a grand time.

We had plans to go on the lake in Munir's boat, but got carried away talking and playing cards. I wanted to go to Pokagon State Park on a nostalgic pilgrimage. Many many years ago, (was it 1970?) you and I came to the lodge for a weekend. It could have been after we were married in 1968. I know we came without children.

You never saw Munir and Cathy's cottage. It is really nice and cozy. Cathy's artistic touch is evident throughout the place. She's used a lighthouse/nautical theme, including the wallpaper, fixtures, decorations, and bathroom accessories. She has a wonderful artistic flare, as you know.

This group is a strange one. We all have different likes and dislikes. We differ in our adherence to faith and religion, and we differ in politics, as well. But somehow, we have found enough reasons to stick together. I guess thirty years is some kind of record. The strange thing is that individually, we will have difficulty in getting along one-on-one with a particular member. But collectively, at our weekly card game or periodic excursions outside the city, we do get along. We are envied by our friends in Toledo, many of whom would like to tag along with us on these excursions. We have steadfastly turned those requests down.

The group always talked about your hospitality (and still does) whenever it was my turn to host the weekly dinners. They all felt very comfortable with you and you felt comfortable with them. Food was important, and you took time to put out a great spread. But it was the way you welcomed them into our home that struck a cord with them.

I still host but bring the food from the outside. I think the tradition must go on. I always invite Nawaz Chaudhary is an infrequent member who attends very few card games. But he always comes when I ask him, and always brings a dessert. He and his wife are still old-fashioned in that they believe in bringing a gift when they visit someone.

I am going to leave earlier than the group to return home as I have to give a talk at a church this afternoon.

With all my love,
Amjad

OCTOBER 25, 2007

My Dearest Dottie,

Ramadan came to an end October 11 and we celebrated *Eid ul Fitr* on October 12. Monie was home to attend your first annual lecture on October 11 and stayed for *Eid*.

Your lecture went very well. The College of Nursing had scheduled two events: one at noon on the Health Science Campus (the former Medical College of Ohio) and an evening presentation at the Hilton Hotel. Melodie Chenevert, a nurse and a motivational speaker, gave both presentations. UT President Dr. Lloyd Jacobs spoke at the evening event. Both events were very well attended. Many of your friends came, except Ann Baker who was out of town for her daughter's wedding. But she sent a most beautiful flower arrangement to our home. It was very nice of her.

The speaker made her grand entrance dressed as a queen. The whole theme was that nurses are queens, and they have to take their proper role in the delivery of health care. She was funny and amusing and interjected an element of "vaudeville" in what the audience expected to be a serious and scholarly presentation. Tasha and I are going to meet with Jeri Milstead, dean of the college, to evaluate the event and make changes for future events. I would have preferred a serious and scholarly presentation.

Tasha also spoke at the evening program, and she was brief, focused and very eloquent. Overall, the first Dorothy Hussain Distinguished Lecture was a great success. After the program, our family and close friends had dinner at the Hilton.

The next day was *Eid*. Monie and I went for prayers. Nothing unusual: the usual sermon, president's remarks and chaotic breakfast in the social hall. As usual, after meeting and greeting as many people as we could, we left and later went to Rehana and Naveed's home for lunch.

Qarie's play opened at the Purple Rose Theater the same evening. Monie and I went to your brother's home in Chelsea for dinner, where your sister, Kim, her husband Tony, and Max and Sherry Planks were invited, and surprisingly, so were Jeff Daniels' parents. The play was funny, hilarious, and wonderful. Our son was at his best and has had some excellent reviews in the papers. After the play we met Jeff Daniels (he founded the theater) and his wife. What a delightful occasion it was.

Your granddaughter continues to mature into a charming and beautiful young lady. It seems like she grows an inch every day. She has turned into a very avid and competent volleyball player. Gone are the clumsy days when she had difficulty in sports. Now she is extremely coordinated and graceful. One of my biggest regrets after your passing was that you would not be able to see Hannah come of age. Talk about the precious and intimate bond the two of you had.

Kevin II [K-2] is still being two, which he is, but he seems to enjoy being rambunctious. His speech is still slow. Everyone assures us that it is delayed and will develop in due time. His tests are OK, otherwise.

I am at peace with myself, most of the time. But occasionally I am not and that distress usually surfaces in dreams. Last week, I dreamed I was at home and in a very angry and agitated state. I went from room to room, screaming obscenities and lashing out. I went into the yard picking up pillows and blankets scattered over the lawn, and moving furniture still on the lawn after last year's picnic. And when I came inside, I saw a swarm of hornets come through the sliding kitchen door. There were cobwebs everywhere. I was scared, and didn't know what was happening. In the dream, I called our friend Naveed to come over and spend the night with me. I was just too dysfunctional and incapable of taking care of things.

I finally woke up in a daze, not knowing where I was. For a moment I thought I was in Peshawar. (Funny, whenever there are doubts in my subconscious mind, it takes me to Peshawar for solace.)

They say dreams are the subconscious manifestation of our state of mind. Although I feel at peace most of the time, there must still be a big hole in my heart and mind that is just as fresh as it was a year ago on December 2. How long will it take? I don't know. But I do know I will work through it. After all, your loving grace is with me all the time, and my dreams are but a manifestation of that tremendous loss.

So console me and look after me as best you can. If there is another dimension where departed souls exist, I wish I could reach over and touch you, even if for a fleeting moment.

I love you.
Amjad

P.S. In a few days, I leave for Peshawar for three weeks to attend our niece Mona's (Dr. Sara Munawar) wedding. Monie is going to join me for a week.

PESHAWAR AIRPORT-PAKISTAN
NOVEMBER 15, 2007, 3 A.M.

My Dearest Dottie,

After a whirlwind three-week visit to Peshawar, I am sitting in the lounge waiting for my flight to Doha in the Gulf and then onward journey home.

When I was leaving home three weeks ago, I left a note for you under the pillow on your side of the bed. I knew you would not be reading it but I did that out of habit. I had always written you a note/letter before leaving for overseas. Most of those notes were to reiterate my feelings for you and how much I appreciated your love and understanding. I will look under the pillow when I get back home in two days. And what a shock it would be if I find the note missing. Would that mean you had read it and had placed it with all the other notes that I had written to you over the years?

My stay in Peshawar was busy and hectic. Soon after my arrival, I attended the wedding of Mustafa Shah, the son of my cousin Sabir. It was significant and important because it was the first happy occasion in their house since the horrible accident of Mustafa's younger brother six years ago. The young man remains in a vegetative state and is being cared for at home.

By the time our niece Mona's wedding came around a week later, Monie had arrived from Los Angeles. The wedding was beautiful and almost perfect. The festivities started a week earlier, and every night we had a gathering at my sister's home, where Monie and I stayed. We had just a great time celebrating the event. Food was served around midnight and the teenagers danced and had fun until the wee hours of the morning. As you know, I can't keep up with that hectic pace. While most of the household slept until afternoon, I had to be out in the morning for my teaching duties at the university or visiting people.

Monie's presence made my stay in Peshawar much more enjoyable and satisfying. We took some time off from family engagements and had a few excursions of our own. One memorable excursion was a train ride to Attock, fifty miles from Peshawar, where we explored the 150-year-old bridge that spans the Indus River. The trains still use it but, because there is a new bridge upstream, all vehicular traffic on the old bridge has stopped. Only pedestrians, usually villagers from the opposite banks, cross the old bridge. We had fun walking the railroad tracks on the upper tier.

We also took walks within the old walled city of Peshawar. I showed him the city as I had known it all my life. Salman Rasheed, a travel-journalist friend from Lahore, joined us on our excursions in the city. Both of them were fascinated by the rich and layered history of this ancient city.

Mona's wedding was a bittersweet occasion. Bitter because she was not only moving out of her home, she was moving away from the city as well. Her husband works in Manchester, England, and she will be leaving with him in a week. But on the whole, it was a very happy and festive occasion. Beego could not have been happier or more radiant.

Monie left a few days after the wedding, and I spent the rest of my time in a hyper-busy state. I needed to catch up on what I had postponed because of Monie's presence. There were a few lectures at the medical college and Lady Reading Hospital, meetings at the new Khyber Medical University as well as the medical university that also bears the name Khyber. I had planned to come back to Peshawar for three months in the spring to teach, but with my appointment to the UT Board of Trustees, I will be able to come but only for one month. The university and college administration are eager and excited to have me come for one month of structured teaching.

I visited Islamabad once to visit our friends Nasim Ashraf and his wife Aseela and had lunch with them. You were part of our conversation. I have observed that women tend to be very sensitive, kind, considerate, and compassionate. While the husbands may not find the appropriate words to inquire how I was doing, the wives always find time and words to ask. Aseela asked and I told her what was happening in my life, and how I was trying to adjust. I had the same kind of caring and compassionate inquiry from Dolores Ali, wife of my friend Mohsin Ali, when I visited them a few months ago in Pinehurst, N.C. Men are as concerned, but somehow it is hard for them to show their soft side.

President Pervez Musharraf imposed a state of emergency in Pakistan two weeks ago, and the whole country has been going through a rather difficult time. There have been mass arrests; all private TV channels (including CNN and the BBC) are off the air. I contacted John Block to inquire if there was some interest in my filing reports for *The Blade*. "Of course," he said. So in the past three weeks, I sent three reports from here, along with pictures. Having gotten used to writing opinion pieces, I find it is hard to limit myself to strictly reporting. Anyway, it was a good exercise.

The Blade also did a wonderful profile on Qarie and the Purple Rose Theater play. It was a very complimentary piece.

I am torn between two worlds. I long to come to Peshawar, but when I spend some time here, I long to go back to Toledo. This is not unlike the process Mr. H. M. Close, my English professor at Islamia College, went through. He had lived in Peshawar since 1947 and considered Peshawar his home. During his biennial visits to England, he would long for Peshawar. But as he grew older, the tug of England grew stronger, and he longed to go back there. In the end, he died in Peshawar but his body was returned to England for burial in accordance with his wishes. Our friend Daud Kamal—Professor of English at the University of Peshawar and a poet extraordinary—wrote this poem "Anchors" which remains in my mind.

Anchor your dreams,
Neither in stars, nor in the sea,
But in the earth,
Where ancestral dust sharpens,
The taste of ultimate dream.

In so many ways, Peshawar has become a strange place for me now, but my abiding love is there. And I still feel the strong pull of the dusty and dirty labrynthine streets of this city.

They've just announced boarding for our flight. I beg your leave as I embark upon the long and arduous journey to Toledo. By the time I reach home, it will be thirty hours from now, and I will be bone tired. I do plan to visit you as soon as I get home.

With all my love,
Amjad

November 27, 2007

My Dearest Dottie,

I have been back home for twelve days now. As I get older, the jet lag is more and more intractable and troublesome. I don't know if it was the jet lag or the fast approaching anniversary of your passing that has been keeping me restless and on the edge. I guess it has to be the combination of both.

It was soothing, however, to sleep in my own bed, our bed. Reflexively, I checked the note I had left under your pillow ... it was still there. What a disappointment. But the gentle sag in the mattress on your side of the bed is still there. That impression reminds me of a poem that my friend Satyapal Anand shared with me a few months ago. We both are going through a similar process. He lost his wife a few years ago. I had not met her but had talked to her on the phone on many occasions. She was born in Peshawar on the street of gold merchants, and migrated to India at the time of partition. Here is the poem he sent to me:

Snow Angel

When the night has deepened
A blanket of silence
Holds me in its tight vice grip
Bundles me up in the bed like an embryo.
Folds and creases

Of the snow-white sheet
Grasp me firmly in their iron grip
Bound I am to the bed
At least for the night.

A light imprint on my right
A slight indentation is all I have of you
A snow angel's imprint
Of the body you've taken with you.

Scared I am of losing it
I lie on the left side
Lest the mark of your body
The snow angel's dimpled imprint is erased
And I am left alone.
If that happens
With whom shall I talk in the dead of the night?

This week has been awfully difficult. I have periods of restlessness, and the only time I am not restless is when I am asleep. And even in that state, my sleep is erratic. Sometimes bizarre and awkward dreams punctuate my sleep. No nightmares, just jumbled fragments of our life together cobbled together in incoherent and hard-to-understand sequences.

Thanksgiving was good and soothing and made us very upbeat. This was the first time in a long while that all our children were here. So were your family, Naveed Ahmed's, and a score of other guests.

We talked about last Thanksgiving. How you were so nauseated that even the thought of food made you retch and vomit. But you insisted on having Thanksgiving at our home. You stayed in the bedroom, and we tried as much as we could to seal off the bedroom from the rest of the house so you would not smell the food. We had our usual sit-down dinner, for forty-five people, aware that you were in the house, but unable to join us.

After dinner, we were all sitting in the living room when you emerged from the bedroom holding your IV pole, wearing striped hospital pajamas, and with a big smile on your face. It's no exaggeration to say that you lit up the room. For an hour, you talked, laughed, and just entertained everyone. Your best laugh line was how you'd feigned illness to get out of the kitchen and let others do the work.

This year, the void was palpable and visible when we gathered in the living room after dinner. You would have been so proud of our daughter. I think she has matured beyond words and has taken charge with comfort and ease that is refreshing, although not very surprising.

My mind keeps going back to your last hospital stay after Thanksgiving. To think about it is to relive the ordeal ... Tasha, your brother Ed and his wife Barbara spending the day at the hospital ... your sister Kim clearing her hectic schedule to be with you. Your sister Sue did not come, although she was informed. She and her boyfriend showed up a day after you had already left us. If it were up to me, I would sever contact, but our daughter and your family have a lot of patience. I admit I don't.

So last week was a time for lots of introspection. I pondered my roller coaster ride this past year, the upheavals, joy and tears, emotions alternating as if I were playing tragic and comic roles simultaneously, to both my amusement and anger.

A recurrent question still bedevils me: Was there anything we could have done to change the outcome? At times these "what ifs" are like volleys of arrows. I have gone over the events, time and time again, and I always come away with the feeling that the dye was cast well before we knew it, and that it was just the question of time. Four years may seem like a long time, but it really was not.

A few people did take note of the Thanksgiving holiday and called me. Your physician and our friend Dr. Kewal Mahajan called to reminisce and to say he was thinking of you. It was very sweet of him.

It is difficult without you. Need I tell you that?

Yours,
Amjad

DECEMBER 3, 2007

My Dearest Dottie,

It has been a year—one whole year—without you. As I lay in bed last night, I had the same empty feeling that I had a year ago when the funeral home people took you, and I felt so lonely and empty. Last night, I also lay in bed thinking about you and the past year. In a strange, and a bit scary, sleep/wakeful cycle, I relived the pain and horror.

It is strange. One would think that seeing you suffer (and you did suffer, often in silence), that the end would be a moment of comfort as your pain was no more. But I guess in real life it doesn't work that way. While you were ill, my energies were spent getting the best treatment possible. Then, when the situation got hopeless, my energies were devoted to taking care of your pain, restlessness and nausea. I was running full throttle on adrenaline. When you were gone, everything came crashing down, and I was a lonely person surrounded by a large crowd.

I am again using sleeping pills to help me sleep through the night. Sometimes I think I am using a chemical crutch to get only temporary reprieve because things are just the same when I wake up.

Yesterday morning, after a restless and sleepless night, I went to the mosque for early morning prayers. There were a handful of people for the service. They were surprised to see me and inquired if I was OK. What could I say? So I said, "Yes, I am fine." From there I went to the cemetery. It was still dark; I sat on the bench and had a good cry. What is there to do except to shed tears of immense loss? As I sat there, the roses I scattered on the grave looked bizarre in bitter cold. They looked like an unrealistic and weird surreal painting of Salvador Dali. I knew that by daybreak, the ever-vigilant cemetery staff would remove the flowers, but for those moments, they made sense, even as bizarre as they looked.

I had toyed with the idea of having a gathering and prayers at the first anniversary, but knowing how you hated the spotlight, I decided not to.

My column on the first anniversary was published today in *The Blade*. There has been a torrent of e-mails and several phone calls. It is difficult to write about personal matters, but I wanted to share my experience with others, particularly with those who are suffering in silence.

There is this sixty-five-year-old widower who, after fifteen years, is still living a life of despondency, preoccupied with the loss of his wife. While there is a tendency on the part of us humans to grow passive and let our mind and environment dictate our future course, that is not a viable option for me. I don't want to crawl into a cocoon or become a hermit.

This past year I have tried, some say very successfully, to stay outside the cocoon. But it ain't easy.

I have not changed much in the house, nor do I want to. This house and the way it is decorated link me to you and I am reluctant to change that. I know sooner or later, I will have to start living in the present and will have my surroundings reflect that. But for now, the sameness is rather soothing.

I am at a loss for words at this time (did I hear you chuckle at my absurd statement?) There is so much I want to talk about, but my mind is clogged and cluttered, preventing the flow of ideas and words.

Perhaps some other time I will be more coherent and interesting.

With all my love,
Amjad

December 27, 2007

My Dearest Dottie,

Christmas came and went. No, it was not a non-event. We were all home. Qarie had just finished the *The Poetry of Pizza* run, and Monie flew in a few days before Christmas. As planned, Tasha and her family came to stay for a few days. It was quiet and meaningful to be with each other on this day. You always made sure the family was together, and we are trying to keep up the tradition. We exchanged gifts as has been our tradition. I was at a loss to buy gifts for everyone. You know how inept I am at buying gifts so gift certificates came in handy. Monie got a big one towards buying stuff for his new home. Qarie also got one to put towards for his new computer. Tasha and her family got token gift certificates, but I am going to pay for their vacation in the coming year. Needless to say, dinner was also vintage Dottie with turkey, prime rib, and the trimmings.

While we were opening gifts in the living room, a large Christmas tree ornament came crashing down and broke with a loud noise. We were startled, but then laughed out loud saying it must be you. How could a large ornament, well-anchored to the tree, slip off by itself? If it were you, you must have liked the congregation of your family around the hearth. We were convinced it was you. One question: Could you have not dropped an unbreakable ornament? But then, it would not have made such a big bang.

There are days when I do feel your presence near me. It calms me and brings me a lot of comfort. But being a man of science, I am always looking for tangible evidence and concrete proof. And I also know that we can't perceive, let alone view, that extra dimension which is the realm of the spirits, ghosts, goblins, and what not. How does one penetrate the invisible barrier short of crossing over?

Elisabeth Kübler-Ross, the famous author of *On Death and Dying*, was reported to have gone in that direction in her later years and supposedly communicated with her dead son. Maybe hidden in what supposedly rational people call mumbo jumbo, there are clues and hints to guide us to that extra dimension. For now, I am content with the feeling that you are around me, and at times, I have the overwhelming feeling of your presence.

I have not been to our cottage on Lake Diane in a few months. I just don't have the heart to be there by myself. A few weeks ago I invited Naveed and Rehana to go with me. We spent a weekend there which was really enjoyable. But I am seriously thinking of getting rid of the cottage. I won't rush, though, and do hope I have a change of heart, so I could spend a day or two there by myself. After all, it was a wonderful refuge for us, one we would steal away to for a night during the week and rejuvenate our spirits. I hope I will be able to do that again.

When I do go to the cottage, I always visit our Amish neighbors, the Henry Delagrade family. They are very kind and hospitable and often I stay for a cup of coffee with them. They talk about you with great fondness.

The new year is upon us. In four days, we will usher in 2008. I wonder what this year has in store for me?

Yours as always,
Amjad

JANUARY 17, 2008

My Dearest Dottie,

New Year's came and went, a humdrum time. I did, however, accept an invitation from Ron Shapiro and his girlfriend Tina for New Year's Eve party. I left their home early to go to Nasr Khan's home in Perrysburg. Nasr had gathered the usual Perrysburg crowd with a sprinkling of Indians. Half an hour before midnight, I took their leave and went over to our daughter's home and brought in the New Year with Qarie, Tasha, and Kevin. Hannah was at her friend Mary's next door. They all came running across the lawn at midnight to wish us Happy New Year. Children are so innocent and precious. Who couldn't feel the lifting of spirits in hearing a child giggle and laugh?

I had not realized the work for the UT Board of Trustees would be so time-consuming. I receive an enormous amount of material, which I try to read, but I do fall behind. I think it is a full time commitment, or should I say a full time job without compensation. But despite that, I am enjoying it. I hope to be able to learn enough in the coming year or two to start making some real contribution. At the present, I acquaint myself with the issues and do the best I can.

I am really excited about the prospects of the university. I believe it has a great potential if we could only induce our local people to think of their university, not as a municipal college (as it once was), but one of the important universities in the state. I am convinced UT President Jacobs is well-suited to lead the institution to the next level.

I invited my poet friend Mohsin Ehsan and his wife Sarwat to come for the weekend. They are staying with relatives in Syracuse, New York. I arranged a poetry recital in their honor at our home, to which about forty-five people came. Mohsin read his poetry and the audience was spellbound. At this time, he is one of the pre-eminent Urdu language poets in the world. His poetry reflects his beautiful personality—charming, low-keyed, and deep. It was a great event, and everyone appeared to have enjoyed the evening. The next day, I took them to the cottage with the intention of staying the night, but Sarwat was uncomfortable staying in a place in the "wilderness." So we came back to the "safety" and comfort of our home.

When Mohsin and Sarwat were visiting, we talked about you a lot. Do you remember when we were visiting Peshawar one year and they had invited us for dinner? After dinner, the conversation drifted to English literature. One of the guests (a show-off, I think) asked me the status of the English novel in America. I do not know much about contemporary English novels and did not know how to answer him. Just for amusement, I said, "Perhaps Dottie could answer that question." You gave me a dirty look because I'd put you on the spot, but you answered him nonetheless. You said, you were not familiar with major trends because you read only a few selected authors, and you then discussed their work. It was impressive, but you were mad at me for putting you in the middle of it. As it turned out, you did wonderfully well.

The literary sittings at our home in Maumee are now assuming a pattern. I invite not more than fifty people, the same number, whether it is inside the house or outside on the patio. Tasha and Rehana arrange for dessert and green tea. Guests also bring, as our friends are prone to do, dessert and sweets. We listen to poetry for an hour or so and then break for half an hour. The second session is shorter, and I ask poets from within the community to read their work as well. A few are OK, but some are depressingly terrible.

I intend to continue the tradition. It brings a lot of joy to me and also to the invited guests. As you used to say, everyone wants to have a good time and enjoys such cultural events, but very few want to go through the trouble of organizing them. How true. But then someone with passion for literature will have to do it.

It is getting very cold outside, bitter cold to be realistic. The house is warm and comforting, and the fireplaces are extremely soothing.

I love you.
Amjad

FEBRUARY 19, 2008

My Dearest Dottie,

Valentine's Day came and went. While we were never very particular about celebrating this day or that day, Valentine's Day was rather special for me for one reason: you did not have to reciprocate. Feeling rather low the evening before, I went to the florist but found the store closed. They did let me in, and I bought two large bouquets for the two special women in my life, Tasha and Hannah. On Valentine's Day itself, however, I kept myself busy on purpose. Other than that, it was an uneventful day.

I am thinking of going to Peshawar for the month of March. Last year when I was there, I committed to return in the spring to teach at my alma mater, Khyber Medical College. I was a bit hesitant because of political turmoil in Pakistan. There have been a score of suicide bombings in Peshawar and surrounding areas. Elections took place there yesterday, and to my surprise and delight, President Musharraf's party was blown away. If things calm down in the next few days, I will make the journey. When I was in Peshawar, I had requested accommodations on the campus because I wanted to spend time close to the students. But because of the political uncertainty, I would most likely stay with Beego in the city. Her home is comforting and safe.

At one time, I thought I was a man of two different worlds, where I could be at ease and comfortable in the U.S. or in Pakistan. Of late I have been having doubts about my versatility. When I am in Pakistan, I enjoy myself for a while, but I get bored and restless and want to come home to Ohio to my comfortable and comforting surroundings. And while here at home I long for Peshawar. I can't tell if one urge is greater than the other. In many ways, I feel like my English professor H. M. Close, of whom I spoke earlier. He was a confirmed bachelor and thus "dropped anchor" when and where he wished. In my case, we had a shared life of thirty-eight years, so without you, I am adrift in my thoughts and my indecisiveness doesn't help. Why life is so cruel and merciless? I will never know.

When I am in Peshawar, the large number of people around me overwhelms me. They mean well, but it is hard to be like an Energizer Bunny. And back home, I am lonely. I want to share the evenings with someone. Friends and family are wonderful, but they can't fill the overwhelming void that I feel when I am alone by myself.

I am still grieving fourteen months later. My public demeanor gives an impression that I have come to terms with the change in my life. Oh, appearances can be so deceiving and misleading. Only very few people know that I am still struggling, still floundering, still hoping and still wishing to turn back the clock.

I think a bit of grief is good for us. It sharpens our intellect and makes us more sensitive to the misfortunes of others. Grief is like sand in an oyster. A few grains turn into a precious gem, but too much of the same kills the animal. I know I have more than a few grains of grief, and at times, I am overwhelmed. Would it be enough to kill me? I don't know … I hope not.

I am seriously thinking of extending my circle of friends to include a few women. It will be good for me to have an occasional coffee or dinner with one of them. It will be new (and scary), but I need to get out of my mind-set and try it.

Last week, Saleh Jabarin came over for dinner. What I lacked in variety of food and a lavish spread (Dottie's typical table), I made up for by having a beautifully set table with china, cloth napkins, and glittering silverware. We sat till late talking about our lives without our wives. His wife, also Dorothy, has been gone three and a half years. In many ways, he is still struggling with his loss. Saleh is such a private person; he seldom if ever, opens up to others. I guess he has made an exception in my case. He still can't see himself dating or seeing women friends outside of work. On the other hand, I have always had women friends.

He asked me if I would ever consider getting married again. Yes, I told him, I do not rule out that possibility. He can't imagine doing that.

But it is hard to find a half-compatible partner. Do you remember, many years ago we were having a conversation with a group of friends and the discussion meandered from subject to subject and finally settled on how spouses have to make adjustments to each other. I said that I don't think I would want to go through the process again, because it is so hard. You were a bit testy that evening. You thought it seemed as if I were unhappy in our marriage. I had to reassure you that in order to reach a comfort level with each other, we both had to work very hard. And while we had achieved a semblance of success, I didn't believe I was capable of going through that process again. And here I find myself facing the same dilemma!

I wonder if they make ready-made wives. They don't have to be made to order, but should be programmed so the adjustment time can be cut to a few months rather than a few decades. Unfortunately for me (and fortunately for the woman) the reverse is also true. How about her anxiety and her concern about hitching up with a man who may turn out to be boorish and uncouth? Pray tell, how do you solve this riddle?

I am sure in days to come, I will write more about this. So let me talk about some other issues that have been bearing hard on my mind. Even with all these friends and acquaintances, I do feel lonely in the sense that I am not able to talk about many things with the freedom I had with you.

I have been rather incoherent in this letter. I promise to be more coherent in my future letters.

I do miss your soothing touch.
Amjad

FEBRUARY 23, 2008

My Dearest Dottie,

Today, a melancholy mood overcame me. Actually this has been happening more often of late, but today was the worst. I want to kick something really, really hard. Hard enough to break my foot, but again I can't. I want to run amuck outside and scream at anything and everything. But again, I can't, and instead I sit here in the living room, brooding and reflecting.

The yo-yo swings, the ups and downs, are troublesome. However, if the truth be known, they are not as severe or as intense as what I went through in the past year. Talk about blue moods—those were the blackest of the black and so opaque you could not see anything through them. It was like a black fog enveloping my whole being.

Of late, I have been thinking of my friends. As we change, our relationships also change. Take Nisar Ahmed in England, for example. He is his usual reserved self. I wish he would be a little more supportive, but that is the way he is. He is not a talkative person, brevity being his hallmark, but I need him to be more communicative. But I know he is incapable of that. Still I consider him one of my best friends. Then there is Siraj. He does call me every now and then and inquires about my well-being. I tell him I am doing well and he is satisfied. I really can't complain about him. He is a trustworthy friend, generous to a fault. He and Munawar have been very considerate.

Alaf Khan is another friend. For the past six months, he has been occupied with his own illness and I didn't expect him to be attentive to me. But I guess he is also changing, as we all do. For the past few years, he has become more sedentary, as if he has lost part of his drive, his zest for life. That man could do anything once; now he is reluctant to drive. So I need to accept all such changes in my friends, as they so graciously accepted me, with all my quirks and idiosyncrasies.

Our card group is doing well. My friendship with them is on a different level and is different with individual members. And of course, Naveed and Rehana remain the mainstay of my support.

I have not heard from my friend Karim [Abdul] in a long time. The last time was when he called to offer his condolences. Somehow we have drifted away from each other. After his wife Nasira died a number of years ago, he married a lady from Lahore. She is, I think, a school teacher. But Karim has rediscovered religion; given his scatterbrained demeanor he can be extremely judgmental of others. I just don't wish to be around people who are so self-righteous.

I always envied Karim for his marriage. Nasira was a wonderful lady. I never found her upset or angry. She was always upbeat, smiling, and lighthearted. Karim used to pinch her butt when she least expected it, and at times when she thought no one was watching, she would show her mock disgust — but with an approving smile.

I enjoyed doing the same to you, but in private. I did not dare do something like that in front of others. Except ... once.

Now, I know you would blush and would be embarrassed, but I must tell this story. It was back in the 1980s, when we went with Bob and Karen Wolf, and John and Linda Mattoni for a weeklong boat cruise in the Bahamas. We were eating dinner one night, when John wanted to take pictures. I gave him my camera to take a picture and when everyone was anticipating a click, I shoved my hand in your blouse and cupped your you-know-what. You were embarrassed, but because you were a good sport, you laughed at it. I don't think you ever showed that picture to our friends when we showed the pictures of our trip. It still brings a smile to my face.

I am getting tired of winter. It has not been a bad one this year, but still I want sunshine and warmth outdoors. I haven't been to the cottage in over a month. I should go and look the place over. I still don't know what I am going to do with it down the road. It is really depressing to see the domino effect of your departure on so many things.

Last week, Dr. and Mrs. John Howard invited me to talk to the residents of Swan Creek Retirement Village. The Howards are staying there for the winter. Both of them have been sick this past year. Sara had an accident and broke a few bones, while John had some breathing problems. They were in bad shape, but slowly and gradually they pulled through and were doing well until a week ago when Sara fell again and broke her humerus. Poor lady.

There were about 100-120 people in attendance for the lecture. They told me it was the biggest lecture crowd they have had. Dr. Howard introduced me and was very pleased with my presentation. I chose the provocative topic, "Why Is Islam So Violent?" I guess it was that catchy topic that brought out so many residents. Some of them came in wheelchairs and a lot of them had their strollers, the kind people use for balance and stability while walking.

My mood is not that blue anymore. Talking to you is always helpful. I will write again. Have you given a thought to dropping me a line? It would scare the hell out of me, but I would love it.

With all my love,
Amjad

FEBRUARY 27, 2008

My Dearest Billo,

For some reason, the name *Billo* came to mind when I sat down to write. In the early years of our marriage, I used to call you that. It is a term of endearment, a distorted version of *billi*, meaning cat in Urdu. Somehow I stopped using it a long long time ago. So here it is again, my dear cat.

I have always felt uncomfortable going to a restaurant by myself; somehow it doesn't look natural to me. So I have been eating totally unbalanced meals at home. They fulfill a purpose and satisfy a need. But when I have some one over for dinner (Saleh Jabarin was the last guest), I set the table in the dining room with cloth napkins to match the tablecloth and place settings of good china. Guests are surprised but enjoy it nevertheless. Earlier in the week Naveed and Rehana came over. I got Italian food from Carrabba's and we had a delightful meal and conversation.

Now weeks go by, even months, before I have something on the stove to cook. I still don't know how to cook. Instead of making an unappetizing mess and frustrating myself, I rely on leftovers and snacks. I have always enjoyed good food but have never longed for it. So my current attitude is not something new or alarming. Friends and acquaintances ask what I do for meals. It is surprising that for many a prepared meal in the evening is the most important thing in the world. Some cynic had once said that good Lord has given us a few pleasures in life, the second of which is eating. Nobody has ever asked me about the first pleasure.

So a few days ago while driving home from the university, I stopped at the Big Boy restaurant at Heatherdowns Boulevard and Byrne Road. Hesitantly, I walked in and felt totally awkward ordering food and then eating alone; there were even other solo diners in the restaurant. I didn't tell this to Tasha, our dear daughter, because she would have insisted I come every evening for dinner to her home. If I resisted her offer, she would stock my refrigerator with all kinds of food.

What I miss the most about food is the aroma when it's being cooked in the house. All the years that we were together, I could smell the aroma in the garage before even setting foot inside the house. The wonderful aroma of basmati rice and stir-fry would even permeate the neighborhood. And then once in a while, say every few weeks, you would really surprise me and cook deep fried spicy *chapli kabobs*. Now I could smell that intoxicating aroma before I had the chance to get out of the car. Then I would see the electric skillet in the breezeway between the house and the garage, confirming my hunch. You always fried them in breezeway to spare the inside of the house from the lingering and sometime intractable spicy smell.

I haven't had *chapli kabobs* this past year, except when I visited Peshawar. They make them in Peshawar the way they ought to be made. I really think you got the knack and perfected the recipe.

FEBRUARY 29

An interesting phone call from Peshawar has brought a host of mixed feelings. The chief secretary of the Northwest Frontier Province

[NWFP], the top bureaucrat, called me out of nowhere to tell me that I was under consideration for the position of vice chancellor of University of Peshawar. I said I was not looking for a job and that I had not applied for one either. He said he knew that but, as chair of the search committee, he would like to add my name to the short list of cadidates.

Now that is enough to shake a rather stable person. I was overwhelmed by the enormity of this possibility.

The University of Peshawar is the oldest university in the North-West Frontier Province. In 1953, as an undergraduate, I saw it taking shape from from the wasteland east of Islamia College. Today, it has ten constituent colleges, about sixty departments, and a student body of 20,000.

I guess they are in the process of looking at some possible candidates from outside the university but I don't know who suggested my name.

I shared the possibility with Tasha and Monie. They both were pleased but I know deep down, they wish it would not happen. And a part of me wishes that, too. But then another part of me wants to do something for Peshawar and the NWFP in the twilight of my life. It is a great challenge with lots of possibilities. I know if we had stayed in Peshawar in the 1970s, I would have headed the medical college and possibly the university. Higher education in public institutions is in horrible shape in Pakistan. I have always had ideas and plans for higher education in Peshawar.

Just imagine if I had a free hand and resources. This university could be transformed into one of the premier universities in the country. The vice chancellor could start exchange programs with foreign universities, get alumni involved, and begin to establish endowed chairs. The possibilities are limitless.

But I am also a realist. I know my limitations and the hurdles one faces in running a university in Pakistan in general, and Peshawar in particular. Maurice Maeterlinck, the Belgian playwright and 1911 Nobel laureate in literature, said something very important about the difficulties in the way of progress. He wrote:

"At every crossway on the road that leads to the future, (tradition) has placed, against each of us, ten thousand men to guard the past."

I am quite aware of the ten thousand men guarding the past and enforcing the status quo. Some of my friends want me to go for it, even if only for a short time. Their idea is that at least my name will be added to the rolls of the men who headed the University of Peshawar. I strongly disagree. If I would take the job, I want to accept it for good reasons and not for becoming one more "has-been" with his picture on the wall.

Do you know how much I miss you at times like these?

In the next week, I leave for Peshawar. I will know more about this when I get there. I will be carrying your sweet memories with me when I land.

With all my love,
Amjad

MARCH 4, 2008

My Dearest Dottie,

A few days ago, I moderated the cancer conference at St. Charles Mercy Hospital. As you know, I do that on the first Monday of every month. It gives me an opportunity to visit the place where I practiced for over thirty years and to renew my acquaintance with the staff.

On this particular day, one of the cases was a borderline ovarian tumor, the kind you had. It was a typical scenario. A woman in her fifties develops the disease and despite treatment, succumbs to it in a few years. What piqued my interest was the statement by a few oncologists that borderline tumor of the ovary is a relatively benign disease and that most women with the disease have over a ninety-five percent survival rate, or even cure. I felt sick on hearing that kind of optimistic but unrealistic outlook. So my dear, you were in that less than three percent who do succumb to the disease.

In reality, I don't believe those statistics. They are in many ways self-delusional. Your disease was diagnosed as borderline, but at the time of the diagnosis, it had already spread in the abdomen. The consultants at the Cleveland Clinic and the Mayo Clinic said it shouldn't be treated at that stage. I am still trying to find that ninety-five percent in all this mumbo jumbo. As some cynic once said, "Statistics are patients with their tears wiped away."

All such discussion does nothing but create doubts in our minds. This "what if" question nags us constantly. But then I have to come to terms with it, irrespective of rosy statistics put forward by overly optimistic and somewhat naïve doctors.

I am leaving in a few days for Peshawar to spend three weeks teaching at Khyber Medical College. My UT Board of Trustees appointment means I can't leave for the previously planned three months, hence the abbreviated three weeks. But I am going to spend as much time at the college and the hospitals as possible.

I also look forward to being there during the very brief spring. You know how intoxicating it is. Amidst all the pollution and urban decay, there are still areas of beauty and unparalleled charm. The University of Peshawar, and Islamia College in particular, come alive in the spring. With orange blossoms all over the lush green campus, every breath takes in the fragrance. I am so looking forward to that.

It is March, but it has been the most bizarre March I can remember. Toledo and the rest of the Midwest are still in the clutches of winter. It snowed heavily these past few days. I do look forward to leaving this white slushy mess behind.

At the card game, Naveed was adamantly against the idea of my accepting the job in Peshawar. Munir was for it, while the others were in between.

In another week I should be in Peshawar, and will know more. This is heavy stuff though.

With all my love,
Amjad

PESHAWAR, PAKISTAN
MARCH 26, 2008

My Dearest Dottie,

I have been in my (and in some ways yours) favorite city for the past three weeks. It was touch and go until the last two days before I left. Peshawar has been in the grip of religious violence and there have been scores of suicidal bombings in and around the city. Before leaving, the question was if I wanted to take the risk to come for the visit. In the end, I decided to come, and I am glad I did.

It has been busy here. As soon as I arrived, I was involved in teaching at the medical college. I must have been jet-lagged when I sat down with the dean and surgery professors to chart my schedule. By the time I wind up my stay here, I will have given a total of thirty classroom lectures and bed-side demonstrations. I am teaching at the dental college, the medical college and all the three teaching hospitals. This is a rather heavy load but I have enjoyed it immensely. I think Pakistan's Higher Education Commission got its money's worth by engaging me to teach. It is gratifying to have students who are eager to learn.

The vice chancellor's job is still up in the air. After I arrived, I let the powers that be know I was in town. A week later, I and six other candidates were invited for tea with the selection committee. I must admit they treated me with considerable courtesy and respect. I was amused by the comments of the other candidates though. Each one was trying his best (no female candidates) to outdo others in one-up-manship. What amazed me was their inability to speak grammatically correct English. There were some who did speak well, but the majority were in the mold of our late friend, Professor Farzand Ali Durrani, the archeologist and former vice chancellor. His English was endearing.

Since that interview, there has not been any official response, but the tug of war for the job has started in earnest on the pages of many newspapers. One letter to the editor said I did not qualify because I was not a professor or retired professor, which is a prerequisite for the appointment of a vice-chancellor.

My remarks to the selection committee were brief and general. I told them I am not looking for a job, but if I am offered the job, and if I think I could do it, then I will consider it an honor to serve. I also informed them that I don't accept a challenge unless I am convinced I can do the job. I think they were impressed, but you never know.

I had told the chief secretary that I would have to look at the university and learn more about it before making any decisions. The next day, I went to see the interim vice-chancellor, who has been in the job for the past six months. Although he expected to be appointed on a permanent basis, he was not included in the short list.

He was a bitter man whose anger was very obvious and palpable. He advised me not to accept the job because it was not worth my time or effort. I wondered why it was worth his time and effort. What a disappointing meeting I had with him. I think he was genuinely threatened by my inclusion on the list. There'd been a rumor he was accused of misappropriation of funds and that was why he was not considered for the job. The saga of vice-chancellorship is ongoing and will unfold at the regular slow agonizing pace that this country is used to.

Peshawar remains enchanting, exhilarating, frustrating, agonizing and suffocating all at once. I try to stay clear of what frustrates me, but it's just not possible. As you know, I am very particular about being on time. So you can imagine my frustration when students continue to enter the class at 8:30 a.m. for an eight o'clock lecture. I told them about it a few times, but nothing changed. So I let it go. I could have put my foot down and locked the door at eight and taught the few students who ventured in on time. If I were here full time, I could have done that, but not as a visitor. Being late is a genetic disorder afflicting a majority of people in the Third World. But I can't, for the life of me, do genetic engineering to fix it.

The afternoon tea on the terrace is still the most favorite pastime for Beego and me and any others in the household who happen to be around, including, of course, the children. With kids riding their bicycles and Osman (Monie) and Shah Mir trying to fly kites, it is a wonderful chaos. We listen to music on my laptop, and when the muezzin from the mosque calls for sunset and early evening prayers, we shut the music off. The problem is that the call for prayers starts from a distant mosque and is repeated, uninterrupted, by tens of other mosques in the neighborhood. The wind carries the amplified sound from the distant mosques, and out of respect, we keep our music off for the duration. After the first wave has ended, we barely have forty-five minutes when the second wave for evening prayers starts. That takes another half an hour to complete. Still we do look forward to our time on the terrace.

One person missing this year was Koko Jan, the elderly lady who lives next door to Beego. She has gone totally blind and has had more health problems in the recent months, including a fall while going down the stairs. She did not break anything but was badly bruised and confined to bed for some time. One day, assisted by our grandnieces, Maryann and Hira, she came through the door connecting the terraces of our two houses. One can go to five or six houses through those doors, and sometimes windows, without setting foot in the street below. Koko Jan had tea with us. She has become extremely forgetful. She asked about you a few times even though on my previous visits, she had expressed her profound sadness on your passing. It was good to see her and share a cup of tea with her.

APRIL 5
DOHA, QATAR

After my whirlwind stay in Peshawar, I flew to Lahore to catch a flight to Doha on my way home. In Lahore, I visited and had dinner with Shamshad Ahmad, the former secretary of foreign affairs and Pakistani ambassador to the United Nations. (We attended his son Faisal's wedding in upstate New York about ten years ago.) He and his wife were gracious hosts. This was the first time I had met them since your passage. They were very caring and talked about you with extreme kindness. Everyone who has met you and particularly those who stayed at our home, do reflect upon their experiences and talk about your superb hospitality.

Before leaving Peshawar, I also met the provincial governor. He, as chancellor of all universities in the province, appoints the vice-chancellors. He wanted to talk to me. For forty-five minutes, we talked about a variety of subjects including my (and his) ideas about higher education. We also talked about the pros and cons of bringing someone like me from the outside versus in-house candidates. I made it rather clear that I would accept the job only if I thought I could make a difference. I also told him that even if he offers me the job, I would not be able to start for another five months. He was surprised. I told him that I have teaching commitments at The University of Toledo that I would like to finish. And there is my Board of Trustees membership from which I would have to resign or take a leave of absence. I did tell him that if he was looking for someone to start soon, I am not the person.

So let us see what he ends up doing. I am excited about the prospect, but I also have serious and grave reservations. Other than the total politicization of the university, I am also concerned about the right-wing religious fanatics who would make any excuse to get rid of a moderate person. As such a moderate, I think my effectiveness would be limited. Another concern, a distant concern, is that my moderate to liberal religious views are a matter of record. Those views are not palatable to the bearded orthodox crowd. Some self-righteous militants can justify anything, including murder, if it satisfies their narrow view of religion.

My flight to the U.S. (and home) leaves in one hour. So long, my love.

I love you with my heart and soul.
Amjad

APRIL 20, 2008

Dearest Dottie,

The visit to Peshawar has created turmoil for me and by extension for our children (and some friends). I need to make a fast and quick decision if I want to serve as vice-chancellor of the University of Peshawar. I am sure I will make the decision after weighing all factors, pros and cons; I just want to tell you "it ain't easy!"

I am at the Providence, R.I. airport, waiting for my flight back home. I came the day before to join Tasha and her family in Connecticut at her sister-in-law Kate's home in Madison. The reason for our visit was to attend the memorial service for Ron Cowie's wife Lisa, at their home by the sea. She died almost eight weeks ago of overwhelming sepsis at the young and tender age of thirty-five. Qarie had flown from London for the occasion. It was a perfect day—sunny, cloudless, bright, and full of hope and optimism. The ceremony was in the garden, with about 200 people attending, many from Toledo and many others with a Toledo connection.

It was Lisa's day in the sun, but I could not resist thinking about you and that our fortieth wedding anniversary would be in a day. We had thirty-eight years together (not counting a few years of premarital friendship) when you left. I saw couples, young and not too young, holding hands and reaffirming their togetherness, while witnessing the untimely passage of a beautiful and vivacious young woman.

Ron told me he understood how I felt. I didn't want to take away his loss by saying yes, we are in the same boat. Instead, I told him that I was given some time to prepare myself (are you ever prepared for such eventuality?) but he wasn't. It was a lightening bolt from nowhere that took his wife away and altered his life forever.

As time passes, it becomes easier at one level, but the prospect of living my life alone horrifies me. I am not a solitary person who would be happy in his own company. But I don't know where to turn. A good companion is not something you mail-order or pickup at the local retail store. Then there are the problems of two cultures. How do you find someone who is at ease in both worlds? It took us many years to forge that comfortable and comforting balance. I have not found anyone except few women, married at that, who are as comfortable as you were. But I must continue to look. And I must verbalize my needs to those who are close to me and dear to me. Reluctance to broach the subject is always there. I don't know how to overcome this "bashfulness," if that is what one calls it.

MAY 19

A month has passed since I wrote the above lines. It was not so much my busy schedule, as it was a sense of apathy and helplessness. There is a reluctance to write, to express, to unburden my mind of the crushing weight of intense loneliness. No matter how busy I get, there are always moments of solitude that weigh me down. The large void that you left is still there. Its sharp edges have smoothened a bit, but the big gaping hole is always there. Sometimes I feel I am being swallowed by it. I tiptoe around its edges, wondering what lies at the depth of the dark black hole.

I am going to stop writing these letters, at least for now. Not that I don't have anything else to say, for I do, but because I feel pretty good about my life on the whole. I also wish there was some response from you, for if there had been one, I would go on for the rest of my days. Perhaps I would get some response if I could travel back in time, just as Christopher Reeve did in the movie *Somewhere in Time*.

I have thought about the amusing possibility of going back in time and staying there, reliving the lived life over again. If I were given an opportunity to relive my life, I would not change the script or the characters except to be more understanding and to have more fun with you. Oh well, it seems a moot point now. But do remember you will always be my Jane Seymour.

So my love, rest in peace, wherever you are and whatever dimension you are in. You know deep in your heart that I love you and will continue to do so for the remaining days of my life.

Until then, I remain yours as always.
Amjad

PITTSBURGH

DECEMBER 5, 2008

My Dearest Dottie,

I thought the last letter was the final letter I would write to you. But somehow I have this urge to continue writing. So I am writing this letter, the last one—at least for the moment—to share other news and views that might be of interest to you.

I am writing this letter from a rest stop on the Pennsylvania Turnpike. I am on way to see our friends Jack and Jill Spooner who, you will recall, moved to West Virginia. We had hosted a dinner in their honor at Navy Bistro in Toledo.

This is long-awaited and long-promised visit. On the way, I am going to stop at John Block's home in Pittsburgh for lunch. John has been my great supporter at *The Blade*. I guess when you own the newspaper, you can have anyone you want on its pages. In my case, he not only took a chance fifteen years ago by offering me a spot on the op-ed pages, but also neutralized the muted protests by his own staff. After all, they must have reasoned, what makes a physician qualified to write for the op-ed pages of a daily newspaper? I believe the passage of time has mollified the skeptics. And surprisingly, I do get, on occasions, a complimentary note from various people at *The Blade*.

A lot happened in the first year of your absence that I haven't written about. Somehow I never told you about the home invasion that occurred last year in May. A black man with a ski mask materialized in my study one night close to midnight. He demanded money, and while I tried to get up from the chair, he sprayed me with pepper spray. When I tried to answer him, he lunged at me with a pistol. I ducked and he pistol-whipped me on the head, leaving a big gash on the scalp.

149

Then he asked me if there were other people in the house. Yes, I told him, my two adults sons were sleeping upstairs. He turned around, still training the gun on me, went to the study door, and yelled to his accomplices to secure the upstairs. As he turned his back to talk to them, I stole away through the back door onto the deck, climbed down the deck and ran across the front yard to the neighbors. I reckon it was not more than five seconds between when he turned his back and I made my escape. By the time police arrived, the intruders had made a hurried exit, taking nothing but my peace of mind. The gash on my head bled profusely because of blood-thinning medicines I take. After spending the night in the hospital, I came home.

It has taken me almost six months to recover emotionally from the ordeal. I have installed motion-detecting lights outside, have made sure all windows upstairs are secure, and have made a habit of securing all the doors at night and turning on the security alarm. They were able to get in because I had not secured the kitchen door that leads outside to the patio. And before you have a heart attack, sit down so I can tell you some more news. (Isn't it silly to ask you to sit down? You are most likely floating around like a cloud.)

I now have a dog. She is a three-year-old, charcoal-colored Labrador. Her name is Sookie, and she is well-trained and very well-behaved. She keeps me company. I still can't bear to have her on our bed and thus she is not allowed to come into the bedroom. She sleeps at the threshold of the bedroom door. Her bark is rather loud but mercifully, she has no bite. It is quite a bit of work taking care of an animal, and while I get frustrated at times, I am managing well.

There is a Persian saying that if you do not have any worries, get yourself a goat. I am finding out that dogs are as demanding and engaging as a goat.

I am healing well. Now whenever you come up during family conversations, and that still happens very frequently, the words are not forlorn and the tone is not sad. It is love, plain and simple, interspersed with jokes and reminescences about the fun times we all had together.

I have been thinking a lot about how I should spend the rest of my life. We'd believed we would grow old together but that was not to be. I am scared to get married. It takes a lot of effort to get to know someone brand new. I do not think I have the stamina or the patience to enter into that unknown. In old age, one needs someone with whom one has shared memories. I cannot imagine starting a new life with a clean slate.

But I am not averse to entering into a friendship with someone who is compatible and shares some of my interests. It would be wonderful to have such a person to travel with and spend time with. There are so many places I want to visit—all those places we had planned to go like Alaska, New Zealand, Australia, the Poles, India. Talking of India, I still cannot get over how much you wanted to see the Taj Mahal, but a pigeon-headed bureaucrat at the Indian consulate in New York stamped our passport with the notation "visa applied for," which in bureaucratic lingo means "visa denied." It took two years to get the stamp invalidated, but then it was too late for you to travel.

Our kids are doing fine. Tasha is working for Regional Growth Partnership as a vice president and director of a division. This is an outfit helping with economic development in northwest Ohio. She is now serving on the advisory boards of the UT College of Business Administration and the College of Medicine. She is also teaching as a part-time instructor in the College of Business Administration. That daughter of ours is full of grace, wisdom, and drive. The tables have turned—now I am referred to as Tasha's dad.

Our granddaughter Hannah, the apple of your eye, is growing into a graceful and poised young lady. She is thirteen but is much more mature than her age. She is smart and intelligent and is always in the top of her class. You did such a great job getting her started on the right path.

Little Kevin, aka K-2, is four years old now. He is a bit hyperactive but is a sweet little boy. And he has a great sense of humor. Recently, he was busy playing with one of his new toy cars when I called him. He ignored me but when I repeatedly tried to draw his attention, he looked up and asked, "Are you talking to me?" Who would not melt with such an innocent and mischievous answer? Beego fell in love with him when she saw him last summer during her visit here.

Our son-in-law Kevin, aka K-1, also never fails to amaze me. He is his usual sweet, caring, and loving self. (I think this sweetness he passed on to his son.) There is nothing he will not do for me or the family. My Pakistani family took an instant liking to him when they were here last summer.

Qarie has finally moved back home from London where he had been living for the past fifteen years. I know you wanted him to come back to the U.S. but he had to make up his own mind. Currently he is on stage doing Tennesee Williams's *A Streetcar Named Desire* at the Purple Rose Theater, and after the run ends, he will look for work here in the states. He has received rave reviews for his role. We all went to see him after the play opened in mid-January. We had dinner at your brother Ed's home. Barbara is such a terrific cook and a gracious hostess. Having dinner at their home beats eating at the Common Grill, the top-rated Chelsea restaurant! After dinner, they accompanied us to the play. It was a delightful evening to say the least.

Monie continues to do well in his not-so-slow climb up the ladder at Allergan, the pharmaceutical company. He makes it to Toledo every six weeks or so, and I am very pleased that he puts in such an effort to come home. Yes, he is still single. I have told these two brothers that as a Pakistani father, I am obligated to host a feast at their weddings.

But I cannot wait indefinitely and the statute of limitations is running out.

Over the past few years, I have become very fond of your friend Ann Baker. I have had ample opportunities to interact with her. My respect and admiration for her has increased exponentially. She has been instrumental in wading through bureaucratic tangles and an occasional incompetence to get the visiting lectureship that we started in your name off the ground and functioning smoothly. I admit I did not know her that well then but am pleased I do now.

This year, the Academy of Medicine of Toledo returned to Puerto Vallarta for its winter seminar. Lachman and Nanci Chablani and Garry and Penny (Reed) Moran were part of the group. It was so great to have them. They were extremely attentive, insisting that I have dinner with them every evening. Just to tease them, I would ask them to get off my back. They always responded that they have instructions from you not to leave me alone. I would imitate Penny, remembering when after the death of her husband, Ben Reed, she came on the trips but was always reluctant to join us and the Chablanis, fearing that she was imposing. And we would tell her to shut up and join us. This time the shoe was on the other foot, so to speak. But all of us had good humor about it, and we never forgot to remember you and Ben with a toast of your favorite libations.

So you see life goes on, even when I ride what appears to be a perpetual emotional roller coaster. In my highs, I am a six-year-old boy, looking for his deceased father, hoping to find him somewhere and then bring him home.

God knows I prayed so fervently then. If children's prayers were actually answered, as we were assured in no uncertain terms they would be, my father would have come back. I wanted him back to take the pain and agony from my mother's the face. So in my highs, I still hope that you will come back to me and that all this had been a

153

big celestial fuck-up. You will somehow speak to me from across some undefined and unknown abyss. Or perhaps I will be able to contact you, see you, and touch you. If there are other dimensions, then perhaps—with the sheer power of thinking and prayer—I will be able penetrate the invisible wall. Just as in *Somewhere In Time*.

But when I am in my lows, science and biology take over. Science does not leave any room for doubt. When a living being dies, it dies for good and there is no coming back. Science is driven by hard concrete facts even though the arts, literature and religion point towards a bigger, incomprehensible aspect of life. Science is concerned with the knowable and provable. Being a man of science and the arts/religion, you can appreciate my peaks and valleys, my ups and downs.

Science is the relentless pursuit of facts. However, it cannot quantify many things that exist but remain unmeasureable. Most of what philosophers think, artists paint, poets write and musicians play remains unmeasured and unmeasureable by available tools.

So wherever you are, be in peace. I am still hoping against all odds that we will meet again. I am leaving the door to that possibility a little ajar. A wide-open door invites one to enter, even though no one knows what lies beyond. A closed door spells finality with no hope of hearing anything from the other side. So I am leaving the door a bit ajar.

Please do know, you are in my thoughts, in my prayers, and in my heart.
Amjad

EPILOGUE

JANUARY 2012

Human history is replete with tales of loss and lament. Death is a lifelong certainty with which we must contend, starting at the day of our birth. Most religions remind us that, while living in the present, we should also prepare for the life that awaits us in the hereafter. These musings are soothing at times, but the jolt of losing someone near and dear to our hearts sweeps us into unfamiliar territory where confusion, anger and helplessness take over our lives and, at least for a while, make us dysfunctional.

As I write these words, it has been six years since my life and the lives of my children were turned upside down. I was not surprised that the death of Dottie affected us so deeply and so intensely. After all, parting is never easy; the deeper the love and friendship, the more intense the pain and the slower the healing. After every stormy night there is a beautiful dawn and sunrise. During these six years, I have made considerable progress and have turned that elusive corner that appeared so close at times, yet was always a mirage in the distance.

It has been a journey of discovery of sorts. It has helped me to discover my own self in ways that would otherwise have been difficult if not impossible. One may be tempted to say that there is always a silver lining but that may lead to an erroneous assumption that a spouse's loss somehow leads to a better tomorrow. It does not. But in the process of healing, one discovers new meanings of relationships, finds new vistas, and amidst pain and longing, finds some contentment and even some happiness. Macabre and perverse it may sound, but it is true.

The idea of writing these letters came to me in an unusual way. During the first week after Dottie's passing, during a regular prayer service at the mosque I attend, my mind wandered off, as happened frequently then, to look at the fragments of our now broken lives. There were some cherished and precious memories—our travels, the hum-drum routine of everyday life, good times with friends and family, and of course, our disagreements and occasional arguments. But no matter how hard I tried, I could not string them together in a coherent fashion. They were always ragged shards of a shattered life that jolted me back to reality. In this confused state, an idea popped into my head that I should write to Dottie and tell her what was going on in my and our family's lives. This way, I could talk about our life together and the happenings since her passing.

For two years I wrote these letters. Through them, I re-lived a good and happy life. Through these letters, I poured out my heart in ways I could not have done in any other way. Writing was healing and satisfying.

———————

Dottie's death had thrown me in the eye of a storm, the ferocity of which I had never known. During her illness, I often thought about her death. Although it was a difficult thing, to comprehend, at least I thought about it. And I thought, erroneously, that I would be ready when the moment arrived. My mind worked like the mind of a scientist, putting all the evidence on the table and reaching the conclusion that nothing more can be done. In a way, this kind of thought process is no different than conducting a scientific experiment that does not end successfully.

What I had not figured on was that, beyond the cut-and-dried approach, there was a huge emotional element that would overwhelm and sweep away the certainty (and fallacy) of the scientific approach. My task was difficult, to say the least. Not only had I to survive this terrible loss, I had also to be strong and understanding for my children.

Soon I realized that it was not a one-way street. They helped me in ways that would have been unimaginable before the lightening bolt struck. And I had to be a sounding board for their anger, their frustration and their pain.

The past six years have been difficult for all of us. Although we have learned to cope with life without Dottie, she is always in our thoughts and in our conversations. But now we can laugh at life, at ourselves, and at times, even at her. It is strange that in the beginning, a mere mention of her would make us misty-eyed and emotional. Gradually we started to talk without getting emotional. Then we started to laugh.

Our children have matured beyond their years. Tasha has assumed the role of family's matriarch and makes sure we, the boys, are always on the same page. She is the anchor I have relied on for safe moorings whenever an occasional emotional storm strikes. We have been getting together for dinner once or twice at her home every week. If she had her way, I would be at her dinner table every evening.

Tasha is now working in the marketing department at The Andersons, a well-known local agriculture/retail company. Our friend Naveed Ahmed was instrumental is convincing her that The Andersons is a good fit. It has been, so much so that she turned down a promising opportunity at one of the local multinational companies to stay with The Andersons. She likes the atmosphere and the ethics that are the foundation of this Toledo-based company. Her husband Kevin remains a loving and an ever-pleasing husband and son-in-law. He is simply a wonderful man, and it is pleasure to be around him.

Hannah, the apple of Dottie's eye, is now sixteen and has grown into a beautiful young lady. She is smart, poised, and a very together person. We think this is the result of Dottie's spending so much time with her as she was a little girl. Hannah plays volleyball at St. Ursula Academy where she is a sophomore this year. It is really a pleasure to watch her take confident steps towards adulthood. This girl will go places.

Little Kevin, K-2, is six and has turned into a handsome and beautiful boy. He has a mind of his own but still listens, with some firm persuasion, to his parents. He is all boy and is popular at St. Joan of Arc Elementary School where he is in first grade. He has an unbelievable chemistry with his Uncle Qarie. Both light up when they see each other. And Kevin is developing a good sense of humor.

Two years ago, Qarie moved back to Toledo after living in London for fifteen years. Dottie wanted so badly for him to come home but it did not happen before her passage. He has begun work in northwest Ohio and Detroit. In addition, he is a part-time faculty member of the UT theater department. He is currently staying with me and has been good company.

Monie, our youngest, is making great progress at Allergan where now he heads the pharmecutical company's global initiatives. He is engaged to be married this summer. His fiancée, Rebecca [Novack], is a lovely and smart woman from the San Francisco area, and they are deeply in love. He has been coming home as often as he possibly can. Sometimes while flying from the East Coast to California, he will stop here for a night. I guess it is reassuring for him to come home to a familiar and comforting place. And it is also reassuring for the rest of us to have him come to the homestead.

My friends have played a rather big role in our journey of healing. Dottie and I met Naveed and Rehana Ahmed when they came to Toledo, some thirty-five years ago. In good times, and in bad, they have been true and selfless friends. They have extended themselves in ways that only real friends do.

I owe a debt of gratitude to another set of friends. Every Thursday evening, for over thirty years, a group of six friends, all men, have met for an evening of food, fellowship and playing cards. This group includes Naveed Amhed, Jim Adray, Karim Zafar, Munir Ahmad, Bahu Shaikh and occasionally Nick Chaudhary. During Dottie's illness and after her passing, they all, in their own ways, have helped me cope with my loss. For me, those Thursday evening card games provided a temporary refuge from the overwhelming burden of my Dottie's illness and death.

My heart disease has finally caught up with me. Over the past twenty years, since my heart attack in 1991, my UTMC cardiologist Mark Burket has kept me healthy and active. In the past twenty years, I have been able to explore the entire 2,000 miles of the Indus River in Pakistan, and to trek to the source of the river in the Kailash Mountains of western Tibet. And I have continued to play my favorite sport, squash racquets.

Then in October 2010, my disease was found to have progressed to where balloon dilations and stents were no longer the answer. I underwent open-heart surgery that month and made a complete recovery. But that was not the end of my difficulties. Six months later, in March 2011, the grafts started to close down. Timely intervention with balloon angioplasty and stents salvaged four out of the five grafts.

Since then, I have been doing well. My physicians cannot figure out why the grafts began to close. Even the Mayo Clinic, where I went for a consultation, did not have a clear answer to my dilemma. I am, however, very comfortable with the disease and what it has in store for me. After all, the sins of the forefathers are sometimes visited on their descendants. Coronary artery disease is rampant in my family, and it is a rare person who survives beyond fifty.

In many ways, I have moved on from the unsure days of six years ago. I have been able to take charge of my life and my surroundings. The unpredictability of my heart disease aside, I live a full and contented life and think I am whole again. Life offers so many little pleasures, and I partake of them.

I have often thought of Dottie's legacy. Her life and her devotion to family and friends were well known. But she also had a professional life as a critical care nurse. I knew she was highly respected in her professioin and that she was considered by many colleagues to be an ideal nurse.

Her devotion to nursing was exemplary. She was not only an excellent nurse, she was also an unabashed patient advocate. She did not hesitate to talk to anyone, including senior physicians, who were rude or dismissive of patients under their care.

In 1996, at fifty-two, she decided to retire. Her decision was triggered by an incident in the emergency room where she had calculated an incorrect dose for a critically ill patient. She caught her error in time and avoided the mistake. But the incident shook her, and she started contemplating retirement. No amount of reasoning or arguing would make her change her mind. To her, there was no room for errors of omission or commission in the practice of nursing. In the end, she listened only to her own inner voice and retired.

To honor her work as a nurse, my family established the Dorothy Hussain Foundation Distinguished Lectureship at the UT College of Nursing. Every fall, a nurse of national or international repute is invited to give a lecture on a current nursing topic to the faculty and students.

Dottie was an intensely private person who avoided the limelight or any form of attention. She did her work the best way she knew how and brushed off compliments or accolades as frivolous or redundant. It was only after her passing that I realized how deeply her colleagues at the former Medical College of Ohio Hospital [now UTMC] admired her. It was probably for this reason that she was always asked to be the charge nurse in the emergency room, even though she worked only part time. It is all the more surprising and gratifying that UTMC selected her (and two other emergency room related staff, a physican and a paramedic, both also deceased) to be on the newly created Wall of Honor at UTMC.

The riddle of the cycle of life and death is hard to accept and harder still to comprehend. Throughout history, philosophers, prophets and sages have pondered this dilemma and have come up short. For some, it was a life after death that was more promising, and thus departure from this world was but a journey towards that ideal life—a state of nirvana.

For others, like third century BCE Chinese philosopher Zhuang Zhou, the cycle of life and death was a never-ending transformation of matter, from one state to another. Perhaps Lord Byron said it best in *Don Juan:*

Oh, the path is through perplexing ways,
And when it's done we die, you know,
And then ... and then?
I know not what; no more do you.

I was six years old when my father died of a heart attack at age fifty-two. At the time, my mother was only twenty-eight years old, had borne four children, and was pregnant with the fifth. She would, along with other women in the family, function normally during the day, cooking, cleaning, and washing for an extended family of twenty-five members. But at night, every night, I would find her sitting at the edge of the bed, silently weeping.

As a six-year-old child, I could not comprehend the finality of death. I still hoped my father would come back, as he always did after his hunting trips to the mountains. In desparation, I started looking for him in the markets, at festivals, and just about any public place in Peshawar. I badly wanted to bring him home for my mother's sake.

And I prayed for a miracle that somehow he would return.

Despite my fervent prayers and soulful cries, he did not. This was the first big disappointment of my life because I had been led to believe that God loves children, and He always listens to their prayers. Later, I realized with considerable bemusement, that if God really listens to children, then most teachers would be dead.

About a year before she died, Dottie developed paraneoplastic syndrome. In this bizarre biochemical and cellular turmoil, the body recognizes the cancer as an enemy and starts making powerful antibodies against the cancer cells. Then, in a desparate attempt to eliminate this new enemy, these antibodies start attacking the cancer cells and—in a biochemical version of friendly fire—the nervous system and other healthy tissues in the body.

One morning, Dottie woke up with a severe headache and, within a short time, started screaming with excruciating pain and calling her long-deceased mother. She was hospitalized and place on a respirator. Somehow she survived that terrible situation and lived another year, during which we were able to take a few vacations and enjoy family gatherings.

I have often wondered if she recovered because of our prayers or the hard work of her physicians. Perhaps it was both. Yet we had also prayed most fervently for her recovery from the cancer, to no avail. God was very selective in granting our prayerful wishes, just as He was in the case of my father, sixty-eight years ago.

Perhaps it is the hidden skeptic in me who at times, rears his rebellious head and questions the very bedrock of our traditions. Prayers are but wishful things that may help us in a crisis, but they do not alter what is inevitable. A Pashtu language saying says it all:

Paikhe naa tekhtaa nishtaa
There is no escape from the inevitable.

In the grand design of our world, things happen because they are *scientifically ordained*. There are diseases, and there are disasters that happen with frequency, and we cannot wish them away, no matter how hard we try. Or pray.

The letters in this book have played a pivotal role in my difficult journey after Dottie's death. So what does one do with them? Put them on a shelf, to gather dust and become part of the accumulated junk in the attic, that which eventually becomes part of a landfill? Or should they be shared with others? The writer must realize that publicly sharing such writing exposes his most intimate thoughts and parts of his life to total strangers.

Publishing these letters was one of the most difficult decisions I had to make. And I must admit that my children were also conflicted and disagreed among themselves about such a decision. In the end, however, the comments of Tom Barden, general editor of the UT Press, and my dear friend, Samir Abu-Absi (who so generously and graciously edited this manuscript), helped me make the decision. It is a love story, Tom said, and it should be shared with others. He further pointed out that the letters would help bring an undertanding of the grieving process, and healing to those who lose a friend, a spouse, or a dear one.

Obviously, I listened to his sage advice.

COLUMNS PUBLISHED IN *THE BLADE*

DECEMBER 18, 2006
Soulmate touched many with her grace

It is not often that I use this space to talk about people close to me. I beg your indulgence as I pay tribute to my dear friend and soulmate Dottie, who was also my wife of 38 years.

It was 42 years ago that our paths—that of a student nurse from Chelsea, Mich., and that of a surgery resident from Peshawar, Pakistan—crossed at Maumee Valley Hospital in Toledo, Ohio.

It wasn't the proverbial love at first sight. On the contrary, it was the battle of the minds and principles that defined our friendship. She was an idealistic young nurse who placed her profession and its integrity ahead of all other considerations. And I was an impatient young man incapable of distinguishing between ideal patient care and insubordination. In my Pakistani mind, doctors gave orders and nurses carried them out. For that irrepressible girl, things were not that cut and dried. A few years later the man from Mars and the girl from Venus decided to tie the knot.

There could not have been two more incompatible people. In due course, however, religious and cultural differences gave way to mutual love, respect and admiration. That was the mainstay of our life together, and in that milieu we would raise a daughter and two sons.

It was with considerable apprehension that she moved back to Pakistan with me in 1970. After all, when the news of our marriage reached Peshawar, the family had mourned and friends and neighbors had come to offer their condolences. But it took no time at all for the family to welcome and accept the new bride into the clan. For her part, Dottie lived the traditions and established bonds with the family that endured the rest of her life. Knowing my deep emotional attachment to Peshawar, she spent the rest of her life nurturing my yearning for that place and helped me with a score of educational and literary projects for the city.

She joined me on many of my foreign trips, and when she would not or could not travel, she took care of the home and hearth and waited for my return. At times she was apprehensive when I took our boys on expeditions, but she never wavered in her support of what I wanted to do.

It was not, however, the big or glamorous stuff that highlighted our life journey. The mundane everyday little things defined her life and accented our marriage: soccer games, piano recitals, school plays, parent-teacher conferences, daily pick up of our granddaughter Hannah from school and, above all, the gathering of the family around the table at dinner time.

Nursing was her passion and she excelled at it. So it was startling when in 1996, at the age of 52, she decided to call it a day. She had made an error in calculating the dose of a medication but had caught herself in time. That misstep affected her deeply, and she decided to bow out while she was still on top. In her mind there was no room for acts of omission or commission. No persuasion on my part could make her change her mind. She was an idealist and also very stubborn.

As the relentless march of ovarian cancer took its toll, she wished to visit Peshawar just one more time to say farewell to our family. But it was too late. In the end she accepted death with the same quiet dignity that she had embraced life.

On her passing, there was a flow of family friends, relatives and even strangers to our ancestral home in Peshawar. This time they came to pay respects to the American girl who was able to narrow the East-West gap. She had lived seamlessly in two disparate worlds and in the process touched many people with her grace. As Ezra Pound said, the quality of affection, in the end, is in the trace it leaves in the mind. There was plenty of it in Peshawar and Toledo these past two weeks.

Throughout history the prophets, sages and wise men have tried to unravel the mysteries of life and death, mostly in vain, and fell short of explaining the stubborn "why?"

One could rely on science to understand the cannibalistic orgy of cancer consuming the body or playing havoc with the delicate biochemical symphony that makes the music we call life. But there is really no good explanation. Prayers cannot alter what God wills.

"I have no more words," said Rumi, the great 13th century Persian poet, "let the soul speak with the silent articulation of face."

Thank you for listening.

JULY 16, 2007
Putting together pieces of a broken life

It was seven months ago that I entered a new phase in my life when Dottie, my wife and friend of 38 years, passed away. According to conventional wisdom, with each passing day the pain and the longing becomes less and that in due course — does any one really knows what that means? — the sadness and lament would slowly but surely recede in the background and be replaced, bit by slow bit, with happy and cheerful memories of a life spent together and spent well. I am still waiting to turn that ellusive corner.

Hidden from the discerning eyes of the world, there has been a scary and unexplainable turmoil and helplessness that has raged below the apparent tranquility of my everyday life. Only family and close friends could see beyond the exterior façade. This led me to join a support group of eight men at the Hospice of Northwest Ohio. Like me, they were also trying to pick up the pieces and cobble together a new life from the shards of a shattered dream. We met weekly and through streams of tears (tears from the depth of some divine despair, as Lord Tennyson so aptly said) and choked voices we shared our stories with each other. To our surprise we all had a common or similar narrative.

All of us, men from different walks of life and most in the autumn of our lives, were trying to negotiate our unsteady steps through the seemingly unending minefields of sorrow, doubt, lament, anger, betrayal, guilt, and unfulfilled promises. We could not see the light at the end of the long and dark tunnel into which we were thrown by fate. Wrapped up in our own pain and misery, we often forget that there are others who are also experiencing the same uncertainties. Intensity and severity of pain may vary but an open and bleeding wound is just as hard to take.

We all felt utterly lost without our spouses. The feeling of helplessness and hopelessness was overwhelming: the inability to write checks and balance the checkbook, to take care of the house, to entertain, to cook a meal, to iron a shirt or to run the vacuum. Or to deal with the callous and greedy, monopoly-driven world of grave markers and cemetery rules.

We also talked about the ongoing onslaught of unsolicited mail and telemarketers. In my case, despite requests on the contrary, I still receive unsolicited mail in her name and unsolicited phone calls for her. They do not believe me when I tell them she has passed away. I don't think anyone would engineer the death of a spouse to get these pests off their backs. Of late, however, I have been telling them that she has moved away and then give them her new address at the cemetery.

We learnt that some friends and acquaintances could be unpredictable and at times unkind and insulting while expressing their condolences. One extended an open invitation to come to his home for dinner and then went on to lecture on how to get on with my life. In his exuberant naiveté, he compared my loss to his contentious and ugly divorce. Yes, he has moved on since but still harbors a deep contempt of his ex. One man wrote to compare my loss to his when his wife left him for another man. Another invited me to Florida where there are thousands of extremely wealthy widows just waiting for a person like me. And to top it off, one man said he knew exactly how I felt because he had lost his dog recently.

We all bear our own crosses and who is to tell which ones are easy and which ones are not? It is difficult to feel someone else's pain unless you have experienced it yourself. Nevertheless, I remain grateful and indebted to friends and strangers alike for what William Wordsworth called their "nameless, unencumbered acts of kindness and love."

All of us in the support group were adrift on the vast and stormy ocean of grief. Though our individual destinations are different we have, for a while, huddled together to see the storm through. Experts and those who have been through this tell me that such storms almost always pass and there is usually a comforting sunrise at the end of a dark and scary night. I look forward to that dawn.

DECEMBER 3, 2007
Journey difficult after loved one's death

Death anniversaries, especially the first one, are always difficult.
If it were not for the resilience of human spirit and the support of
family and friends, the dark clouds of despair would push many of us
mortals into the throes of deep depression. It is through these tenable
bonds that we face calamities and overcome obstacles.

This is the third column I am writing on the loss of my wife who
passed away a year ago yesterday. At this time of introspection, most
of the world happenings, exciting and intriguing as they may be,
appear remote and distant. I beg your indulgence as I look back at the
roller coaster ride my family and I have endured this past year.

It has been a difficult, and at times painful, journey of adjustment
and understanding. It was made easy and bearable because many of
you wrote and shared your stories. Your individual circumstances
were different but your narratives of loss and lament and hope were
strikingly similar. You helped me see more clearly through the
frightening fog of uncertainty and disbelief.

All of you mentioned the void, a big hole as some of you put it, that
has become part of your being. Not as an outside garment that covers
the exterior but as what Lord Tennyson called the captive void of
noble rage. Passage of time does take away some of the sharp edges
but the void remains.

Nine months ago, when I joined a support group at the Hospice of
Northwest Ohio, the councilors cautioned us to brace ourselves for
an uneven ride on the terrain of our remaining life. They told us that
while in time surface wounds do heal, lurking under the surface,
barely a tiny scratch away, are memories both painful and pleasant.
The sudden appearance of a trigger—the flash of a favorite color, whiff
of a familiar perfume, aroma of freshly baked bread, or a melody

inextricably linked with a long-past romance—opens the floodgates of uncertain emotions. A million reminders, big and small, force one to return to the sad realization that what once was, now is not.

In some ways it has also been an interesting journey. In the deepest of the blue moods—where one is engulfed with uncertainties—there appears, from nowhere it seems, a ray of hope for a better tomorrow. In those moments in my mind's eye, one sees and feels the presence up close but still separated by a mysterious and unknowable abyss.

I can, a year since, look back and realize that death and dying is an awkward situation for most people. We try to camouflage the stark reality with euphuisms and clichés. "She is in a better place," goes one worn-out statement. I am expected to nod my agreement. Instead, to the bewilderment of the consoling person, I say there was nothing wrong with the place she was already at. I am sure, given the choice, she would not have opted to go to that better place.

"It must be God's will," goes another oft-repeated, feel-good cliché. Being a person of faith, I cannot question that without treading on thin theological ice. But in the past year there have been moments, however transitory, when faith and reason have clashed. Some consider faith as a convenient crutch but for others it is indispensable. Lord Tennyson, in his timeless elegy *In Memoriam*, said it eloquently: "By faith and faith alone, embrace/Believing where we cannot prove."

The passage of time and a persistent longing for a departed spouse makes most of us see the person through the prism of emotions, and perceive her to be perfect and the union with her more so. Realities of life, however, tell us otherwise, but we celebrate, just as generations before us, ordinary lives in extraordinary ways. So I mourn and celebrate the life of a woman who considered herself very ordinary but to me, my family, and friends was, in the words of William Wordsworth, "A perfect woman, nobly planned" and "Fair as a star when only one/Is shining in the sky."

When I wrote about Dottie a year ago, I concluded the column by thanking my readers for listening. Now, a year later, I close by thanking you for sharing your stories and helping me understand mine.

I am grateful.

DOTTIE'S CHILDREN REMEMBER THEIR MOTHER

Funeral remarks by Monie Hussain

Good morning, and thank you for coming. I would also like to thank my Uncle Naveed for sharing so much of his perspective on the deep friendship that he and my Auntie Rehanna have shared with both my mother and father over the last thirty years; I would like to share with you a little different perspective on my mom, the kind that is unique to a son or daughter.

I met my mother about thirty-two years ago in Lock Haven, Pennsylvania. In the early years, when I was very young, I can say that my mom was the smartest person on the face of the earth. She not only knew everything, but also everyone. I don't know what happened, but about the time I reached the age of fourteen or fifteen, I realized she had changed. How she didn't always see my brilliance was beyond me. Remarkably, though, she transformed yet again. In fact, she continues to get smarter the older I have gotten.

While that perspective may not be unique (I am sure many of you parents and children alike can relate) my mom's devotion to her family was legendary. As a wife, mother, grandmother, as a sister, a daughter, as an auntie—my mom always put family first. For her own parents (whom you have already heard a little about) she played in important role in their lives up until their last days, visiting them in Chelsea, Mich. nearly every week. My mom had a close relationship with her sister-in-law in Pakistan (whose name appears on your program), and a very special bond with her granddaughter, Hannah, who frequently made those weekly trips to Chelsea with her. This devotion to family was never out of obligation, but out of love. While I suppose I had always known on some level, the last few years have shown me how much that devotion extended beyond out immediate family.

On my frequent trips home to Toledo during the last few years of my mom's illness, I frequently found myself answering the home phone and talking to people I either didn't know (many I had never even met) who were not only calling to see how she was doing, but felt the need to tell me how important my mom was to them. These were people she had met over her lifetime, who shared with me snippets of how she had made an impression on them (and often helped them) at some time in their life—new in town, going through a difficult time or just working alongside her.

Then there was the trip to Pakistan last year. I was truly overwhelmed, again, by the outpouring of love and concern from so many family and friends she had touched some thirty-five years ago, when she, my dad, and my sister and brother lived there. The genuine emotion that has remained over the years and the miles was amazing for me to experience, and served to show me that my mom was important to so many people.

All of you being here today is another example of this to me. You knew my mom from so many places and times—from MCO, ST Vincent's, the Islamic Center, and so many more. Today reminds me that my mom was not just part of my family, but that she created family in whoever she touched. She has left us quite a legacy.

Tasha's reflections on grief and grieving

I

The thing about grieving that no one tells you is that you are actually not part of the living world for a while. You go through the motions of your life, but each movement, each thought, each plan has haziness about it. The sharpness is not there and the color is faded. I suppose that is the same description that a clinically depressed person gives when describing their world. It makes me wonder how long I am supposed to tread water before I can take a deep breath and be wonderfully surprised by life again.

To make up for my handicap, I have found myself exaggerating my appreciation. It's like my poor beat-up car is struggling to get up that steep hill so I press my foot to the gas to give it a little more power, but either the peddle is too touchy or my foot is too heavy. The car jumps and my head is thrown back against the seat, and I find that I have, indeed, moved forward a bit. Panicked, I then jerk my foot off the gas altogether and the car settles to a stop. That is my life lately. I watch the squirrels chasing each other in the backyard and concentrate on how amazing it should be to witness the first signs of spring—that life does go on—and all that stuff. I notice the trees slowly turning green and the blue jay flying through the drab with a shock of color and promise. I know what I should be feeling, but I don't.

I am waiting for my intention and appreciation to meet again and I know that it is dangerous to give up. Going through the motions serves its purpose. It allows me to enter the world of the living again even if I feel like a fraud. When my true spring finally arrives it will come to a wiser, deeper and calmer woman who knows just how gently the peddle should be pushed to make it to the top of the hill.

II

The spring after my mother died, the lilacs in my garden did not bloom. I had planted three bushes seven years before and watched them grow and each year with much pride.

The first year that I planted them, they stood embarrassed, yet hopeful, against the house. The blooms were perfect, like grapes. The weight of the flowers almost bent the small bushes, but you could smell the sweet smell of spring way out by the mailbox in the street, if the wind was right.

By years three and four, the bushes were sturdy and proud. Although the bushes are strong, the blooms only delight for a short time. They appear to introduce spring and then quickly fade, to give way to the flowers of summer elsewhere in the garden. But it is on those few spring mornings that are misty with gentle rain and the air is the prefect temperature—where you can wear either a sweatshirt or a T-shirt and it all feels the same—when the lilacs become magical. The mist in the air holds the scent still in front of you. You don't have to chase it on those mornings. It's a rare moment. You can walk for many feet and the lilac stays with you.

By years five and six, the bushes stood a full four feet above me. The blooms rounded the top and middle and bottom. Those years, I cut enough flowers for my house and my mom's and you couldn't even tell that I'd stolen any. I filled vases so my house smelled like lilacs in every room. My mother and I talked about the flowers those years. We compared notes—are yours wilting? No, not yet. I just love the smell— you know spring is here when the lilacs come out.

My mother died in December. The winter that year was tricky. A warm spell came though right before Christmas and confused the tulips and daffodils and cherry blossoms. Many of them began to blossom, only to be frostbitten. Until then they had been sheltered from the long and cold winters. Until then, their timing had been impeccable. Until then, they had not seen what a horrible place this can be for delicate and hopeful blooms whose only job is to tell us that spring is, indeed, here.

The lilacs did not suffer like those early risers. I know this because the lilac is also wild. I see them on the side of the road—like a fence—beside the cornfields. I see them in the middle of the woods and growing beside the grocery store. The blooms this year seem exceptional to me—except in my own garden. My bushes tower over me but only produced a few bunches of blooms this year, way at the top. I had to stand on a ladder to cut them, but there were so few that I only took two.

They sit in my kitchen in a special vase, but this year I have to bend down to gather the scent. It does not float in the house like the years before. But, if I close my eyes and breathe the bloom deeply I can almost feel the mist in the air and the damp on my skin. I can almost hear her say that this is the best year she has ever seen for lilacs.

III

Sure, grief is personal. Everyone goes through the process in a unique way. Grief is not a timeline, though. It does not follow a straight path where you can be sure—given enough time and distance—that true progress will be made. Grief does not pay attention to such things. Instead, your breath is squeezed out of your body at surprising times. Mundane times. Times when you are dusting or grocery shopping or brushing your teeth before bed. Times when you really hadn't planned to cry and you didn't bring any tissues.

I thought that there would be a catharsis that would relieve the pain and anguish. I pictured a moment sitting at my kitchen table where I would beat my fists and cry so hard that I could not catch my breath. My head would hurt and I would use a hundred tissues. I would babble about the unfairness of life and my misery would hang in the air around me. After a while, my sobs would slow and everything would be still and I would feel lighter and stronger. I would feel peace. I would feel resolve and I would know that I could push through and get on with life little by little. My sadness would not keep me from breathing.

That is not the way it is with grief. It becomes a part of your life, your body. You always own it, a nagging and dull ache. Many days you are busy so you hardly notice. There are those other days where things aren't quite as balanced and it takes over because nothing is there to keep it out.

Horrible, you say? I disagree. You grieve because you loved and this new body part keeps you company. It will forever. Sometimes it is awkward, this prosthetic. You have to get used to something that you did not ask for. You have to learn to walk, to live, to breathe, in a new way. And just like having children and becoming a parent, this thing called grief, this new body part, is something inexplicable to anyone who has not lost something of immeasurable value.

A SHARED NARRATIVE

The Blade readers' feedback on Dr. Hussain's three columns

Editor's note: As all e-mail writers know, abbreviations, numerals, and short phrases are common in emails and thus have not been corrected here. The writers' personal details have been removed, except from several messages whose writers provided their public identities.

Subject: to Dottie
Date: Tuesday, December 4, 2007
To: <aghaji@buckeye-express.com>

Oh my. What a moving column I read in *The Blade* today. Although I've experienced many personal instances of dying, the loss of your wife seems so much deeper.

I grieve for you and your family.
S. D.

Subject: nice article
Date: Monday, December 3, 2007
To: <aghaji@bex.net>

Dear Dr. Hussain,

I always enjoy reading your articles. I was saddened last year when you wrote about the loss of your wife. Your compassion and love for your wife are clear. I had no idea that I would follow in your footsteps. We said we won the Lottery of Life! In June, I retired as a high school counselor, and our only child was beginning her final year of med school. Bob had back surgery in June. One week later while pumping gas, he was told he had terminal cancer. His oncologist had a great plan which would give him 5 plus years. We knew he could beat it! Two months later he had a PE [pulmonary embolism] and I lost the love of my life. You are an inspiration to me.

Sincerely,
L. B.

Subject: From N
Date: Monday, December 3, 2007
To: Amjad Hussian <aghaji@buckeye-express.com>

 Dear Amjad, I read the column about Dottie with great interest. This was one of your best literary works. Your emotion and feelings were palpable and your insights deep and profound. She may not have liked all this public attention, but she would have approved of the quality of your work.

With warm regards.
N.

Subject: article
Date: Monday, December 3, 2007
To: <aghaji@buckeye-express.com>

Amjad,

Read your article and have to agree. Even tho my wife died 6 years ago
this past Sept, and I have since remarried, there are things and times
when I still think of her and the times we had. After almost 35 years
you just can't replace someone or somethings you had. Brace up, keep
close to family and have a Good Holiday.
R.

Subject: The Difficult Journey
Date: Monday, December 3, 2007
From: Julie Rubini <julie@clairesday.org>
To: <aghaji@bex.net>

Dear Dr. Hussain,

I have enjoyed your various writings for the Blade throughout these
last several years, and my heart went out to you when you shared the
news of your wife's death.

After reading your tribute to her and the process of grieving her loss,
I felt compelled to write to you.

You brought a tear to my eye as you shared the roller coaster ride of
emotions and experiences over the last year. I remember, and still
experience those moments myself. My husband and I lost our oldest
daughter, Claire, seven years ago. On the heels of this great tragedy
my older sister, Karen, died nearly four years ago. We miss them
both dearly, and like you, remember them well, and celebrate their
lives and memory often. We've created an event in Claire's memory,

Claire's Day, which is held at the Maumee library every third Saturday in May. It's proven to be a very healthy and good way on which to focus our grief energy.

More so than the wonderful joy that we bring to families in the community in Claire's memory and honor, I'm most proud of how we've continued to celebrate life with our two other children, and each other. As we attended bereavement support groups in the earliest, darkest days after her death, we saw too many families that not only lost a child, but lost their relationships with each other as well. I would not stand for that, and neither would Claire.

I really appreciated your comment about the clichéd statement, "She's in a better place," as I replied pretty much the same as you; Claire was in a pretty good place here with us as it was. The other comment made at the funeral home (I filed this one in the dumb and stupid things people say, when they truly only mean well) was that "God must have wanted her more!" He must have wanted her pretty bad, too, as she was loved very much here on this earth.

Thank you for sharing your grief and your pain. My loss is different than yours, and some might say greater, although losing Brad would be devastating, and selfishly I secretly pray that we both die together to spare each other the loss of the other.

You reflected on this very difficult year, and so very accurately described the pain, and yes, even the joy that comes with the territory.

Thanks for sharing.

Sincerely,
Julie K. Rubini

Subject: Thank you
Date: Tuesday, December 4, 2007
To: <aghaji@bex.net>

Dr. Hussain,

Your articles regarding your wife have truly touched the hearts of many in the area. Thank you for sharing your experience and your personal feelings.
L. S.

Subject: your Dec 3 column
Date: Tuesday, December 4, 2007
To: <aghaji@buckeye-express.com>

Hi Dr. Hussain,

Bev told me that you were in the SC library last week.
I'm so glad for your safe return from travel.

Your column about Dottie brought tears. I'm sorry for your loss and glad you can share the grief with family and friends. My mother in law told me that she should have joined a grief support group, because other people just don't understand the experience.

Thanks for your gift of teaching. I may be able to speak my sympathy more acceptably, by learning from you.
G.

Subject: Blade article
Date: Tuesday, December 4, 2007
To: "S. Amjad Hussain" <aghaji@bex.net>

Dear Dr. Hussain,

Once again you have piqued the hearts of your readers. I didn't get
a chance to read yesterday's Blade until I was at school waiting for
my study group to meet. I read your article and a flood of emotion
came over me. It has been a little over two years since my husband
died and I can tell you that though my meltdowns happen much
less frequently, they do still occur. I agree that there are a million
reminders of one's lost love, and the ever haunting realization that
that part of life is over is as painful as ever. You are also so correct
about the "prism of emotions" through which our memories see
our longed-for one. I still feel guilt when I remember a less-than-
perfect aspect of his personality, as if that point should never again be
assigned to him.

Today was our last day in a critical care class that I took this semester.
Our instructor, Julie Popp, showed a video on death and dying. The
video was very good but more than once it reminded me of the last
few weeks of Jim's life and it was very difficult to watch. I found
myself struggling to hold back tears in a classroom of people who
over the last two years have become my dear friends. Though they
offered consolation, until they have felt the same pain they can't really
understand.

Please know Doctor, that in your writing of your very real pain that
you are still helping others to deal with their struggle. No matter how
far out from our loss we get, we still will always at some time need the
support and comforting words of another who has lost a love.

Your readers are grateful.
Sincerely,
J. H.

Subject: Dec.3...” Journey difficult after loved one's death”
Date: Tuesday, December 4, 2007
To: <aghaji@bex.net>

Dear Dr. Hussain:

Your words really touched me, and I read them over again. In fact, I just had to cut it out and save for future reading. Your wife must have been a most wonderful lady and how blessed you were to share your life with her. My heart goes out to you and all your family as you continue this difficult journey without your loved one.

Respectfully,
C. T.

Subject: Keeping you in thought and prayer...
Date: Monday, December 3, 2007
To: <aghaji@buckeye-express.com>

Salaams Uncle,

In remembering the loss of a loved one, every day can be difficult, but anniversaries can be especially tough. I just wanted to let you know that we miss Aunty Dottie very much and our duas go out to you and your family during this time. Aunty was a wonderful lady and I have fond memories of her that I will cherish forever.

I hope you and the family are doing well, and inshaAllah, I'm planning a trip to Toledo soon to visit.

Love,
W.

Subject: Toledo Blade
Date: Monday, December 3, 2007
To: "aghaji@buckeye-express.com"

Dr. Hussain,

Your article intrigued me today and I wanted to let you know that my mother and her sister lost their mother in May to cancer at the age of 90. When [I am] speaking with my mother and aunt, they still cry to this day. I will be passing along your article along to them in hopes that it will ease their pain to a degree.

Thanks for sharing your personal story.

Best Regards,
D.

Subject: article
Date: Monday, December 3, 2007
To: <aghaji@bex.net>

i rarely read your column but today's title caught my eye. my wife died of cancer at the age of 43, over 5 years ago and i still think of her constantly. i wish you well in your journey without your wife it is not easy or pleasant. if you care to correspond, my home e-mail is ___.

Subject: column
Date: Tuesday, December 4, 2007
To: Amjad Hussain <aghaji@buckeye-express.com>

Salaam Uncle Amjad,

I just read your column and it was quite touching. I especially liked this paragraph:

— The passage of time and a persistent longing for a departed spouse make most of us see the person through the prism of emotions, perceiving her to be perfect and the union with her more so. Realities of life tell us otherwise but we celebrate, just as generations before us, ordinary lives in extraordinary ways. So I mourn and celebrate the life of a woman who considered herself very ordinary, but to me, my family, and friends was, in the words of William Wordsworth, "A perfect woman, nobly planned," and "Fair as a star when only one/Is shining in the sky."

However, from the experiences I have had with Aunt Dottie and the many wonderful stories I have heard over the years, she seemed to live an EXTRAORDINARY life that we can only celebrate in ordinary ways. Speaking from a "younger" perspective, there are certain people who have a "glamour" factor about them and your wife was definitely one of them. It is those types of people who inspire us younger generations.

Hope all is well,
T.

Subject: <no subject>
Date: Monday, December 3, 2007
To: <aghaji@bex.net>

Dr. Hussain,

I just finished reading your article in the *The Blade* about your dear
Dottie. As a wife of 43 years, I can't even imagine the loss you must
feel. Thanks so much for sharing your thoughts and feelings with us.
It's interesting, isn't it—whether we are doctors, clerics, laborers, or
whatever our state may be, the human emotions all run the same,
depending upon our life experiences. I'm so glad you have good
memories. So many can't think back on such happiness.

Peace be unto you and yours.
Sherry

Rev. Sherry Schermbeck, Chaplain
Pastoral Care Department
St. Charles Mercy Hospital

Subject: your Monday December 3rd column
Date: Monday, December 3, 2007
To: <aghaji@bex.net>

Dear Dr. S. Amjad Hussain

Hello, my name is K ... . The reason I am writing, is because I am a
reader of the *Toledo Blade*.

Monday December 3, 2007 I read your column titled Journey difficult
after loved one's death. This column is about the loss of your wife and
the changes that are just supposed to come to you, and without any
control. I love the column, if that's OK to say. It brought back feelings

that I had over the loss of my mother Hazel in Winston-Salem N.C., in December of 2005.

I was working in Toledo then as I still am now, when she passed away. This December 17 it is going to be two years. I wish she was here; she enjoyed life so much because of her five children, along with her five grandchildren. By far things are not perfect now, but I have something now that I didn't have then, and that is Hope.

If I may, Romans 15: 4—"For all the things that were written aforetime were written for our instruction, that through our endurance and through the comfort from the scriptures we might have hope." In your column you used words like death anniversaries, frightening fog of uncertainty and disbelief, unknowable abyss, and the two that a lot of friends said to me—"She is in a better place" and "It must be God's will"—and after these words you tell your readers you have faith. I really do believe you have faith, and hope.

Dr. Hussain, have you ever heard that it's better to be a live dog than a dead lion? Ecclesiastes 9: 4,5: "For as respects whoever is joined to all the living there exists confidence, because a live dog is better off than a dead lion. For the living are conscious that they will die; but as for the dead, they are conscious of nothing at all, neither do they anymore have wages, because the remembrance of them has been forgotten."

I just wanted to tell you what gave me hope, the things that I have come to know from the Bible since the death of my mother. Revelation 21: 3,4: "With that I heard a loud voice from the throne say: 'Look! The tent of God is with mankind, and he will reside with them, and they will be his peoples. And God himself will be with them. And he will wipe out every tear from their eyes, and death will be no more, neither will mourning nor outcry nor pain be anymore, The former things have passed away.' "

Dr. Hussain I also love the Bible account at 2 Kings chapter 4. It is about a woman promised a son who dies at a very young age, and how the boy's mother finds Elisha, a prophet of the true God, so as to ask for her son's life to be given back to him. I do believe that God is going to make all things right, so I feel in my heart down to the very core of my soul that your wife and my mother are awaiting an resurrection, by God's only Begotten son, Jesus Christ. Your column made me stop and think about the past two years of my life; it's not every day that one is able to read something that powerful. It made me think that two years ago I didn't have hope and now I not only have hope for myself but also for others.

Thank you,
K.

Subject: Today's column
Date: Monday, December 3, 2007
To: <aghaji@bex.net>

I read your column today through tears. I lost my husband of 58 years just 5 months ago. Until you've been there the loss is unimaginable. Hospice of Northwest Ohio was and still is a great help. It is a roller coaster. Just when you think you have adjusted to reality a small reminder has you in tears. I share your grief.
E. C.

Subject: Journey.......
Date: Monday, December 3, 2007
To: <aghaji@bex.net>

Dr. Hussain,

In late October I received my husband's cremains and on 17 Nov., I had a graveside service. Frank died June 25, 2005 and following his wishes, his body was donated to MCO. I thought it would give me peace, being able to put him in his place next to our son, allowing me to talk and pray with them together, but instead it was like re-living his death, giving me such a sad feeling of loss. Even my parish priest made light of it, and I turned to another priest who is my friend and with his help I managed to get through it and keep going.

Today is the anniversary of my son's death; the feeling of loss and sadness intensified as this date grew near. On Thursday I also have to face the anniversary of my mother's death. So many loved ones have left me in the past ten years, including my beloved pets.

Ready or not, I have to cope with Christmas. As the chairperson for St. Vincent de Paul Society at Immaculate Conception Church, I am concentrating on making the holidays brighter for those in need in the area of the church, many more are coming with needs this year. Keeping busy with that project helps but even so, the sadness creeps in.

The first anniversary is the hardest but all anniversaries and situations are a constant reminder.

Yes, I've heard all the clichés and ridiculous remarks people make at the time of death, some quite thoughtless, sending me into the deep abyss of depression. I wonder why, asking God for an answer, what have I done to deserve this, often questioning my own faith.

And no, my loved ones are not in a better place. How can death be better than life?
 D. C.

Subject: Re: Journey difficult after loved one's death
Date: Monday, December 3, 2007
To: Dr Hussain <aghaji@bex.net>

Dear Dr. Hussain:

Congratulations on living through what was probably the worst year of your life. You began writing about losing your beloved Dottie a few months after I lost my Phil. In the little over a year since he died, I've learned a lot, mainly that grief cracked me open like a nut, exposing all the soft parts of me I tried to protect. Despite having lost my parents or older relatives and the occasional young one, I never experienced grief in the way I have since Phil's death. Grief has opened me up to feelings I either kept suppressed, as I had been raised to do, or opened me to feelings I didn't know I had. In the last year, I've grieved losses and sorrows from previous decades, along with the loss of Phil.

Phil and I were not married. He was a widower when I met him, and I was five years past a divorce. After the heartbreak of divorce, I finally met a wonderful man. We were both cancer survivors and he was in remission. We met, felt an immediate connection, and became friends, lovers, and companions for three years before lymphoma finally claimed him. "Godamn cancer," he used to call it. We talked on the phone every day, spent three to four days and nights a week together, and supported and loved each other. The most intimate times we spent together were in the last few months of his life when we both knew our time together was too short. His two kids and I were with him in his last hour, and along with hospice, we cared for him in the beautiful log home he had built just two years before.

Grief is a foreign land. None of us willingly buys a ticket for the trip to this sad place, but we all end up going for a long visit at some point in our lives. I'm having trouble leaving this melancholy place and getting back to what I once knew as home. Just when I think I'm outta there, back in the land of the living, something pulls me back and I feel like a pile of poop. I'm nearly 60, I feel useless and irrelevant most of the time. I work as a medical transcriptionist from my home (I implore you, if you still have occasion to dictate, e-nun-c-i-ate!), where I live alone. I force myself to get out. I have friends, children, grandkids. But life just isn't the same since the angel of death finally wrestled Phil to the ground. I've had counseling, done a lot of hospice-recommended reading, but Phil is still gone. He had become a part of my life so quickly and then, he was gone.

I write every day but the urge to publish has gone the way of so much in my life. I had a career once, traveled all the time, and was very creative and energetic. I used to run in races, cross-country ski, hike and camp and had ambitions to hike parts of the Pacific Crest Trail. I feel like that was another person who did all of that. I have been trying to force myself out of my house to volunteer, as I used to do, but even that feels flat. The fizz has gone out of the champagne. Other days, I feel hopeful, get out and do things, connect with others, but then I seem to somehow end up back in the Land of Loss, which is no longer the foreign place to me it once was. I expected the loss of Phil would hurt terribly. I didn't know it would completely knock me off my feet and change my perspective on everything.

In a previous essay, you wrote about the crazy things supposedly well-meaning people say to grieving people. After Phil's death, we were at the funeral home. A friend of ours marched up to me and in front of several people loudly demanded of me, "Now what?" I was momentarily confused and then told her we would leave the funeral home and go to Phil's house to eat. "No! Now what? What are you going to do with the rest of you life?" Now, as then, I have no definitive answer for that question.

For 15 years I lived in East Dearborn, Michigan, the token Hungarian in a Lebanese neighborhood, and in between bites of fattoush and shish tawook, I learned a lot from my neighbors about things other than food. I learned about their beliefs and how they got them and heard a point of view other than that of American mainstream media. Your point of view is always an informative, enjoyable read for me. I'm grateful to you for sharing your personal pain as well as your love of Dottie with your readers.

Sincerely,
G. T.

Subject: Remembrance
Date: Monday, December 3, 2007
To: <aghaji@buckeye-express.com>

Dear Amjad,

Thank you a very moving remembrance in your column today.

November 1 was the anniversary of Maj's passing, and it was a very difficult milestone for me. A gesture by Toni Andrews at the American Gallery in Sylvania helped me. She held a retrospective exhibit of Maj's textile art on loan from those who had purchased the pieces. She also hosted a reception for many of our friends to coincide with the anniversary. I took some photos of the exhibit and posted them on a website at:
http://astro1.panet.utoledo.edu/~ljc/maj_retr.html

I had seen the pieces one at a time, but to see so many of them together at the same time gave me a new appreciation of the diversity of her talent.

I've read a book called *About Alice*, written by Calvin Trillin about his wonderful marriage and ultimate loss. He concludes that his wife would now say, "I've been so lucky," to which he adds "I try to think of it that way too. Some days I can and some days I can't."

I'm glad to see that you have been able to travel and do important and meaningful work. I'm trying to do the same. Some days I can and some days I can't.

All the best,
L.

Subject: thank you
Date: Monday, December 3, 2007
To: <aghaji@buckeye-express.com>

Dear Doctor: I have read many of your even-balanced columns, the latest on the anniversary of the death of your wife. I wish to thank you for your insights. I have been writing to a beautiful and sensitive woman in her 50s, sentenced to a horribly long prison sentence in a federal institution by certainly questionable prosecutorial tactics.

Recently her mother—her closest friend and confidante—died. This lady shared with me the agony and pain of being completely isolated from the event, in a place of near insanity. I have used poetry, understanding and all at my disposal to help her through this, even though I am not a believer in a compassionate creator of such a violent place populated by humans.

But it is columns such as your own that have helped me convey what small sense of justice I have to this torn-apart woman. For that I thank you and hope you continue to write from your own sense of understanding until you no longer can. ...B. H.

Subject: Journey as a spouse
Date: Monday, December 3, 2007
To: <aghaji@bex.net>

I was having my coffee this morning and read your article regarding your journey this past year. My husband passed away Dec. 17 last year, and I find this time of year to be a bit stressful for myself and family. After being married for almost 43 years I find myself at times in a tunnel looking for a way out and, hopefully, will find this new life I didn't expect to be living so soon, a positive journey for me. I do find "triggers" that can put me in tears and haven't found a way around this as I can't control what music stores play, etc.

Just wanted to tell you what you already know, and that is you are not alone on this roller coaster ride and, hopefully, the ride will stop soon and let us get off, at least for a time. I do laugh more and have wonderful support from family and friends, but the void is there. I'm single! Wow, what a word and being a widow doesn't sound much better.

Happy holidays to you and your family.

Subject: Journey
Date: Monday, December 3, 2007
To: <aghaji@bex.net>

Following your articles over the years, I have disagreed with you often. But one thing totally stood out to me.

It was how loving, caring, and what a wonderful nurse your wife was. It makes me warm to think about the love and respect you two have (not "had") for each other. People love the toasty God things to say to each other. I once had a 25-year-old manager working for me who was diagnosed with cancer. My display manager said to me, "Well, you know, God takes the good people first." What junk! I guess I am a bad person as I am still here.

Anyway, you touched on your strength to move on in your article. You must celebrate your wife's life, and not mourn her loss. Celebrate her life. Throw a party in her name. Create a charity to celebrate who she was. You always will have the pictures and memories of her life.

And, as you know from this past year, we all can tell you how to deal with your loss. It's easy to say these things, but so hard to live them.

But, you know, at least people care! I feel your pain.
E. G.

Subject: RE: A personal column
Date: Tuesday, December 4, 2007 11:11 PM
To: <aghaji@buckeye-express.com>

Dr. Sahib:

Our heartfelt condolences to you again, at this difficult time in your life. As believers, we must trust our Lord when He says: *Kullu mun Al'yha Faan* (everything must come to an end). A person of your stature and experience needs no reminder that nothing belongs to us except in memory.

Your emotional writing about her for the past one year tells the readers that she is always with you.

We pray that Almighty bestows peace on you and makes it easy and rewarding for you to live in the shadows of her memory.
A.-M.

Subject: Re: A personal column
Date: Tuesday, December 4, 2007
To: <aghaji@buckeye-express.com>

Thank you for sharing your story, Amjad sahab. I am not going to
say all the other cliches that you have mentioned, but here is a new
one for you: We stay on this earth only till our time is allotted. When
that is up, we are gone to the place where we came from. I can totally
believe you when I read your column ... I feel your pain ... but I also
feel that you are a wonderfully strong man and shall go on writing
your columns and doing constructively positive things till your time
comes to go and meet up with your lovely wife. Like you said, Faith
keeps you going. ... and OF COURSE the column that you write ...
which incidentally ... is cathartic.

A sister who is praying for your strength,
S. A.

Subject: Re: A personal column
Date: Wednesday, December 5, 2007
To: <aghaji@buckeye-express.com>

Your words are truely beautiful am deeply moved. Can't say bravo as
it's about such a deeply sad part of your life, love. And I agree that
even though your wife considered herself to be ordinary, she was
anything but that. May her soul rest in peace, ameen.
B.

Subject: Hello
Date: Wednesday, December 5, 2007
To: <aghaji@bex.net>

Dear Dr. Hussain,

Please allow me to add, belatedly, to those who tell you we understand your pain and loss.

My husband died three years ago, and, if anything, I miss his presence in my life more every day.

Also, please give my best regards to Qarie. Jim and I were in a play with him once, at Village Players. ...*And a Nightingale Sang* had one of the very best ensemble casts I've ever had the privilege of working with. And I have followed Qarie's career with great interest ever since.

I enjoy reading your column regularly.

God bless you,
Pat Rudes

Subject: Thank you
Date: Wednesday, December 5, 2007
To: <aghaji@bex.net>

Dear Dr. Hussain,

Once again thank you for your eloquent piece on grieving. You put into words what I suspect only those who have experienced great, close loss can really know. I feel that you helped some people to say, "Yes! That is how it feels."

I sent your piece to my father, who lost my own mother in Dec. 1955, and my stepmother of 47 years in Dec. 2005. I think he feels that no one really understands, but perhaps your thoughts came close.

My best to you in this time, and may you, too, find some peace.

Sincerely,
D. D.

Subject: Re: A personal column
Date: Wednesday, December 5, 2007
To: <aghaji@buckeye-express.com>

My dear Amjad,

It was a privilege and honour to read and share this column with you. Tears came to my eyes; what can one say? Words will not suffice.

Yes, Wordsworth said it beautifully, "A perfect woman, nobly planned," and "Fair as a star when only one/Is shining in the sky."

And, I also recall Ezra Pound's, "The quality of the affection/In the end/Is in the trace it leaves in the mind."

Affection for her will always be carved in our minds and hearts. May her soul rest in peace. God bless you and all your dear family.

Yours fondly,
M. and D.

P.S. We so look forward to your next visit to serene P____. Soon we hope. Take care. M.A.

Subject: Journey difficult after loved one's death
Date: Wednesday, December 5, 2007
To: <aghaji@buckeye-express.com>

Dear Amjad Sahib,

AOA. I cried after reading your column. I see and do understand the pain people go thru when their loved ones die in my hands despite my best efforts to save them, and the pain B. & I have gone thru on losing our parents over the years. Brother, no one else can feel the actual depth & extent of the pain you are going thru but we see it and know it. This is the law of the nature that we all have to depart sooner or later for an eternal journey.

"kullu nafsin zaiqatul moat" — the Quran
"dust thou art to dust returneth" — the Bible

May Allah help you in your difficult times after loss of your life partner!
M.

Subject: Re: A personal column
Date: Wednesday, December 5, 2007
To: <aghaji@buckeye-express.com>

Dear Amjad,

This is the first thing I read this morning. It brought tears to my eyes. All I can say hope your journey from now on is as easy as God can possibly make it for you. We will pray for your well-being.

I cant believe its been a year. J.

Subject: Re: A Personal Column
Date: Wednesday, December 5, 2007
To: <aghaji@buckeye-express.com>

Assalamualaykum
Dear Dr. Amjad,

Thanks for sharing you feelings with us.

My mother just passed away on Nov 29. I am obviously in the early stages of my grief. She was a very graceful and the most pleasant person that I had ever met, like almost all women of that generation. She was a companion to my father for almost 61 years. My father is very distressed. I had never seen him grieve like this except when his younger brother was killed.

What I'd like to ask you as to what as a child can I do to help him through this time, especially since I live in the U.S. and he is in Pakistan.

Thanks,
R.

Thank you for your kind note.

In our culture we do not verbalize our feelings to our loved ones. Somehow it is understood but never enunciated. I would suggest you make it a point to call your father often enough and tell him you think about him all the time and that you wished you were with him in this difficult time. And if you can, go and spend some time with him in Pakistan. These are the things that will soothe his pain and give him hope.

Regards,
Amjad Hussain

Subject: Greetings.
Date: Wednesday, December 5, 2007
To: Amjad Hussain <aghaji@buckeye-express.com>, and others

Dear Friends,

Yesterday I promised to send you my paper which I shall read on Sunday at Z.'s introduction at Dr. M.'s residence. But comes "Journey difficult after one's death." This very title shook me up as I was aware of the background and see the pain and suffering of deep scars. But after [I read] with teary eyes, the whole column put me at ease.

Amjad has handled this grief remarkably well. He remembers the past, he analyzes present, and remind his friends what he wrote on the same subject a year ago. He considers people saying "She is in a better place" or "It must be God's will," but brushes it off and thinks of his life together at their "own little corner of the world" which is filled with joy and love and memories which he knows and the "better place" he rejects.

There are some heart warming analyses of bygone days such as: "The sudden appearance of triggers, a flash of favorite color, the whiff of a familiar perfume, the aroma of freshly baked bread, a melody inextricably linked with a long past romance open the flood gates of uncertain emotions." He quotes Wordsworth: "A perfect woman nobly planned" and "Fair as a star when only one is shining in the sky."

The column on Dottie's anniversary overall is not all sad, but it is remarkably encouraging for others, those who have experienced such grief, and it shows the inner strength of Amjad. God bless Dottie. You are a remarkable man, Dr. Syed Amjad Hussain.

After this long discussion, I am still enclosing my paper for you to read, hoping it may bring a brief smile on you lips.

Love,
I.

Subject: Hello
Date: Thursday, December 6, 2007
To: <aghaji@bex.net>

Dear Sir,

Assalamualaykum. This is just to pay salaam to you. I know you will be very sad as one year has passed when your beloved has passed away.
Assalamualaykum Jek aur baras beet giya us ke baghair. Jis ke hotay huay hotay they zamanay meray.

Any way, may the Almighty keep you happy and in good health.

Regards
Dr A. S.
KUST Institute of Medical Sciences, Kohat

Subject: WOW
Date: Thursday, December 6, 2007
To: aghaji@buckeye-express.com

Wow, God bless you and thank you for having the courage to share your journey. I lost my brother to suicide six months ago and I can definitely call it a journey. You are right that it is so difficult to talk about death in our society and much harder when it is suicide. Then mix it with militant Islamic fanatics who questioned us burying our brother in an Islamic tradition.

Thank you again for sharing and may all of the prayers give you a greater understanding of life and its complexities and to feel great joy in the moment of such great grief.

Sincerely,
M. S. MD

Dear Dr. S.,

Thank you for sharing your story. It is most unfortunate that we still have to face ignorant religious bigots in the most trying times of our lives. They are the people who have never heard of the healing process after the death of a dear one and are totally oblivious to the physical and mental illnesses that induce us to take our own lives. Compassion for them is an abstract concept.

Please do know that there are people in our tradition who are sick and tired of these so-called custodians of our faith.
Warmest regards,
Amjad Hussain

Subject: Re: A personal column
Date: Thursday, December 6, 2007
To: aghaji@buckeye-express.com>

Dear Dr. Amjad,

Once again, I had a tear in my eye. I marvel at your fortitude, though. I had not expected to see you as spirited as you were in Peshawar. I suppose that is the resilience you mention in the piece. All I can hope is that when my time comes, if it comes at all for who knows which one of us will go first, I have the same courage and resilience. Many thanks for sharing this piece with me. Best regards.
S. R.

Dear S.,

Thank you for your note. I am glad the piece resonated with you.

I function rather well most of the time except on those private moments when the reality overwhelms me. If you could, please send me the pictures of Khans Korner and other relevant images.

As always,
Amjad

Subject: Your Dec. 3, 2007 editorial
Date: Thursday, December 6, 2007
To: <aghaji@bex.net>

Your perspective on death was thought provoking for me since we all wonder how others handle the experience. I especially liked your caption to the article. Somehow it was comforting despite the reminder of the loneliness we live with once we're old and alone. Thank you. I enjoy your articles. Mrs. J. O.

Subject: Salaams
Date: Thursday, December 6, 2007
To: <aghaji@buckeye-express.com>

Dear Dr. Hussain:

Al-salaamu alaikum. We haven't met, but my friend F. D. sent me a recent column that you wrote for the Toledo Blade. I wanted to thank you for that.

My wife died 15 years ago, so I know something of the journey that you are on. All of them are different, of course. Here's something I wrote several years ago, looking back on my wife's death.
Salaams,
Amir Hussain
Department of Theological Studies
Loyola Marymount University

Shannon's Song

Easter, 1998

As a Muslim, I accept the Qur'an to be the very word of God, revealed to the Prophet Muhammad in the seventh century. It is in the words of the Qur'an that I find the themes that are important to me: love and mercy, peace, justice and compassion. At this point in my life, one verse in particular is most meaningful. (The translation from the Arabic original is my own.)

. . . "And God has put between you Love and Mercy.
Truly in this are Signs for those who reflect." (Qur'an 30:21)

Many verses in the Qur'an speak of the "Signs of God," which are everywhere. Trying to understand or decipher these signs is one of the duties incumbent upon all Muslims. As I understand it, the verse speaks of the love and mercy that are found in human relationships, specifically, the relationship between married people (mentioned in the verse immediately prior). And the root or cause of human love and mercy is divine love and divine mercy, two of the attributes of God.

I did not truly begin to understand the many levels of meaning of this verse until I met my wife, Shannon L. Hamm. Shannon was born in Winnipeg and grew up in southern Manitoba, a member of the United Church of Canada. To say that Shannon was the most amazing woman that I had met would be an understatement. She was so involved with the world; she loved to travel, talk, dance and, especially, sing. While I remember her as a singer, she was also a first-rate thinker, the recipient of many academic awards, and a truly gifted teacher, whether working with university students, abused women, mentally handicapped children, or head-injured adults. And she worked with all of these. Shannon and I were married on August 19, 1989. The service we designed included readings from both Christianity and Islam, including a longer passage from the Qur'an that contained the verse above.

Shannon challenged my world, the "know-it-allness" that only a twenty-three-year-old male can have. She taught me about peace and justice and the need to make a difference with our lives. Although she discovered her answers within a Christian framework, she helped me to find my own answers within a Muslim framework. This is important for me to say, because terrible misunderstandings persist about Islam as a religion of violence and Muslims as a violent people, stereotypes which are as destructive for Islam as they are for any other world religion.

As I read the Qur'an, I discovered its overwhelming emphasis on the mercy and compassion of God: the idea that reconciliation and forgiveness are preferable to retribution, that mercy takes precedence over wrath. In addition to the Qur'an, Muslims have the life of the Prophet Muhammad as an example. In reading about his life, I repeatedly encountered images of love and compassion, ranging from everyday acts like playing with his grandchildren, to acts of statesmanship in forgiving those who had persecuted him for the ethical monotheism he preached. And I discovered countless examples in the Muslim tradition of people who practised mercy and justice, people such as Badshah Khan, who worked with Gandhi in using non-violent resistence as a way to end colonial domination in South Asia.

I learned that these teachings of peace and justice were not foreign to Islam, but an integral part of it. To me, this was the secret of interfaith dialogue—not that we seek to convert each other but that we help each other find what is meaningful in our own traditions—that Shannon, as a Christian, could help me to become a better Muslim.

Transformed by my experience with Shannon, I began to do interfaith work, largely, but not exclusively, with the United Church. The challenge to work towards a just society led me to join a number of groups, including the World Conference on Religion and Peace, the World Interfaith Education Association, and Science for Peace. Again, I did all this within a Muslim framework, trying to follow the examples that I had been given from within my own tradition.

And then my world changed.

On July 7, 1992, Shannon died suddenly of a pulmonary embolism. At twenty-six, hers was the first death of someone close to me, and I had no words for it, no models for my grief. At that point, I did not stop believing but I did not know what to believe. I could not reconcile the ideas of a loving and merciful and all-powerful God with a God that would let Shannon die. At her death, Shannon was twenty-eight, the clinical manager of the Centre for Behavioural Rehabilitation, working with people with acquired brain injury. She was the classic example of a wonderful young woman doing important and ground-breaking work. And I could not imagine a God that would let her die, taking her away so quickly from such critical labours.

Of course, I have never been the same since. Shannon's death taught me many things, and in her death, she continues to be one of my teachers. I remember old conversations in different ways, thankful for a teacher who left me with answers to questions I had not yet learned to ask. And while there has been none of the communication with Shannon that I have so desperately sought since her death, occasionally I am blessed with some sense that she is still here. That her song is still being sung, in her own beautiful voice.

One of the times that I heard this song was while offering prayers in the lodge at the Dr. Jessie Saulteaux Resource Centre in Beausejour, Manitoba, in a gathering led by Stan McKay and Janet Sillman. The lodge that day held people from several traditions, and we all prayed together, as well as offered our own prayers in our own languages.

Another time was at a United Church service in Toronto. July 7, 1996, was the fourth anniversary of Shannon's death, and it happened to fall on a Sunday. I had no idea what to do with myself that day. For no conscious reason that I can recall, I decided to go to the church that Shannon sometimes attended in Toronto, Trinity-St.Paul's on Bloor Street. I had never been to a church by myself for no reason before. The minister, Joan Wyatt, was on holiday, and the service was conducted by Michael Cooke, Juliet Huntly, and Sarah Yoon. And everything about that service was connected to Shannon, as if it were her memorial service. We sang one of her favourite hymns, there was a reading from a book she loved, the importance of meaningful work was stressed, and we held hands and danced for the closing hymn. Of course, these people had no knowledge of Shannon, and I had never met any of them prior to that day's service. It was just one of those magical moments.

Despite such moments, I have also come to understand that my faith, my Islam, does not bring me healing. Instead, it does something infinitely more powerful. It allows me to live broken. It allows me to understand something of the gift that is life. As a believer, I know that at some point, Shannon, God, and I will meet again. And I will be asked what I did with this life I was given, what difference I made with that life.

And I have been so incredibly fortunate, to be given a life, and texts for how to live that life, and a teacher to help me read those texts and many more teachers since that first, best teacher. In the fall of 1997, I returned to San Francisco, a city that I had last visited five years before, only months after Shannon's death. Five years later, an important change came over me. As I sat down to a meal with one of my teachers, professor Michel Desjardins of Wilfrid Laurier University, I realized just how many gifts I had been given. The "Why me?" question that I had been asking was still my question; its emphasis, however, was totally different. Instead of "Why me? Why am I so cursed? Why did I no longer have Shannon around?" now the question was "Why me? Why am I so fortunate to be given so many teachers and friends?"

What will I do with all that has been given to me? In my own poor way, I, too, will try to sing Shannon's song. I turned to my favourite complete chapter of the Qur'an (chapter 93), "The Morning," and found solace:

By the morning.
By the night when it is still.
Your Lord has not forsaken you, nor is your Lord displeased
And The Last will be better for you than The First
And your Lord will give you so you will be content
Did your Lord not find you an orphan and shelter you?
And find you erring, and guide you?
And find you needy, and enrich you?
So do not treat the orphan harshly.

Nor drive away the petitioner.
And proclaim the bounty of your Lord.

These words were first given to the Prophet Muhammad and, through him, to all people, myself included. They are the words to Shannon's song. Help people. Work towards justice and mercy in this world. Proclaim the goodness of the Lord.

Let her song be sung.

Subject: (no subject)
Date: Thursday, December 6, 2007
To: <aghaji@bex.net>

Amjad,

I just finished reading your thoughts on the day of Dottie's death anniversary. Your faith is much stronger than mine since mine did not survive after August 1, 1985 when I buried my 23-year-old daughter Aniqa (nickname Bisko) in Lahore. She had died on July 29, 1985 in Pakistan.

Literally killed by a physician ... her fault was that in a bout of depression she had taken over dose of noramitriptyline. A physician in the Mayo Hospital gave her intravenous valium to stop the toxic twitching without ever considering putting her on a ventilator before that, and then walked away. Five minutes later she had a respiratory arrest and left us forever. A very sound choice of treatment could have been doing nothing.

I no longer believe in divine justice nor restitution. In my new faith, we, the human beings, created the heavens and God in our minds to hide behind the intoxicating thoughts that this was his will and this separation is temporary [before] meeting in a better place. We never think twice about crushing to death the ants under our feet without realizing what we have done, although these creature for their size are as much intelligent, sentimental, and family-oriented as we are. Yet we don't think of God raising them and restoring them in heaven, as we pretend he (why not She?) will restore us.

Although in due course, the pain gets dulled or attenuated by the analgesia and amnesia provided by time and other business of the world around us. But this relief is a very thin veneer that gets rubbed off every morning when I wake up or when I suddenly wake up in the middle of the night.

"Ab to Juebar-e-zindagi chup chaap see hai haan kabhi Uthi sadaa-i-dard jub koi kinara kir gayaa."

What I am trying to say is that this pain is eternal. One may not utter a word but inside the hurt of the loss is forever. My father was married to a lady for over 10 years when she died of tuberculosis in 1930. He married my mother in 1934. Many years later I overheard a conversation between my father and mother ... Mother: "who will you ask for, if in the next world? God wanted you to choose an eternal partner." My father's immediate response was "I will ask for TWO."

He must have loved his first wife very much and must never have gotten over the grief of his loss to spontaneously come up with that answer.

I am sharing these few thoughts that are buried deep in my soul since the shared grief may lessen the eternal pain, albeit momentarily.
A. T.

Subject: Re: your aticle in the blade
Date: Friday, December 7, 2007
To: aghaji@buckeye-express.com>

Dr. Hussain:
I work for Skyline exhibits, and worked with you for a very short time on a design project about 7-8 years ago. I don't know if you remember me as J. G.? (It was before I was married).

I had the opportunity to read your article in The Blade on Monday morning. With (3) little children, I don't have much time these days, but I was so grateful that I had a moment to stop and read your aticle. I have to admit, I'm very behind the times. I wasn't aware of your wife's passing last year. I just wanted to let you know that I was very sorry to hear that, and you will continue to be in my thoughts and prayers. I did have the opportunity to meet Dottie, while we were working together, and for the brief times we met, I remember what a warm, kind person she was.

She always made me feel so comfortable when I stopped by the house once or twice to drop off some things. I'm glad that I had the opportunity to meet her.

This time of year is always difficult, especially when you lose someone close to you. After 17 years, I still miss my dad. Sometimes I think I miss him more, now that I have children. I so wish that he could be here to see them. However, I do find comfort in knowing that he has a great view from where he is … and I also know his spirit lives in my children. It amazes me when they will say or do something, that reminds me of him.

I just wanted to let you know that I'll be thinking of you this holiday season and through the new year.

And I hope we have the opportunity to cross paths again.

My best wishes to you,
J. K.

Thank you J., for your very kind note. Life is so unpredictable and fragile.

I do remember you (how could I forget your beautiful smile and your friendly demeanor?) from the mosque project we worked on a number of years ago.

With the help of my family and friends I am doing rather well. I appreciate you took the time to write.

Warmest regards,
Amjad Hussain

Subject: Re: Dottie
Date: Friday, December 7, 2007
To: aghaji@buckeye-express.com>

Hi Amjad,

Hoping that you remember our days at MVH/MCO. I worked in ER with Carol Topliff and with Dottie at times. Anyway, just wanted to tell you that a friend from Toledo sent me the recent article from The Blade dated Dec. 3. What a beautiful article and tribute to our dear friend Dottie. She was "a perfect woman" in every sense of the word. I was so happy that my friend remembered me telling her about you and Dottie and sent me your article.

We live in Holland Mi. now and have since 1974. They have never made us a Wolverine, though, as we are true Scarlet and Gray Buckeyes.

My thoughts and prayers are with you and may you be surrounded by friends and family.

With care and concern,
L. S.

Hello L.,

Thank you for taking the time to write. It was good to hear from you. I trust you are doing well.

Warmest regards,
Amjad

Subject: Re: A personal column
Date: Friday, December 7, 2007
To: <aghaji@buckeye-express.com>

Asalam Alaikum Uncle,

I just wanted to post a comment on how deeply touched and how greatly inspired I was after reading your beautiful column. I still can't believe a year has gone by. I do agree that it is a tremendous help with all the support our close friends, and close community members give to us. I know that whenever I go to visit my papa, I always say a prayer for Aunty Dottie too. She truly was one of my favorites in the community. I looked forward to seeing her in our community gatherings. She is and always will be greatly missed. May Allah continue to bestow his blessings upon you and your family (Ameen). Take care, Uncle.
S.

From the Letters to the Editors (published December 29, 2007)

Amjad Hussein, MD, in the editorial memoir "Journey difficult after loved one's death" (12/03/07) beautifully describes the exquisite and bittersweet feelings experienced after the death of a spouse.

Memories of his wife, Dottie, which were so beautifully articulated in this essay, contrast with the suddenly recurring feelings of grief, loss and emptiness experienced by family and friends during this time of the one-year anniversary of Dottie's death. For me, these feelings of grief are intensified by the behavioral expectations imposed by the holiday season. Dr. Hussain's very human responses help us all feel that we are not alone in experiences of personal grief, however they may relate to us in our own lives.

Dr. Hussain thanks all his many supporters for the "gifts" they have extended by their letters and personal contacts. On the contrary, I thank him for his gift to us—a beautiful tribute to his spouse, our friend, Dottie.
Ann Baker Ph.D., C.N.P.

Date: January 2, 2008
To: aghaji@buckeye-express.com

Dear Mr. Hussain:

I must tell you the Dec column regarding your wife's death of a year ago was almost the exact feelings I have had since April 14, 2007 when my wife H. K. died. She had a very short illness with cancer of the liver and the shock of her passing was quite often reflected in your column.

I have been intending to write you but misplaced that December copy of the Blade and just now in Monday's Dec 31 I found your email address.
Thank you so very, very much for that column … it certainly strengthened my resolve to carry on.
M. K.

Thank you Mr. K__.
The healing process is slow but it does happen. I am sure you have already noticed some reduction in the intensity of your grief. My best wishes are with you.

Regards,
Amjad Hussain

TERMS USED

Aapa:
In Urdu, a big sister. At the time of her marriage, my mother was fourteen, and the other children in the household called her Big Sister. The name stuck and everyone, including her own children, called her Aapa.

APPNA:
Association of Physicians of Pakistani Descent of North America

Assalamu alaykum:
Muslim greeting in Arabic, meaning "peace be on you." Also spelled Asalam alaikum, Al-salaamu alaikum

Billo:
Term of endearment, from the Urdu word billi, meaning "cat"

Chat:
Savory snacks, often made with fried dough, also spelled chaat

Chapli kabobs:
Deep fried spicy beef kabobs that are a delicacy from the frontier areas of Pakistan

Eid ul Fitr:
Celebration at the end of Ramadan

Hindi:
An Indo-European language, resembling Urdu. It is one of two official languages of India but is spoken mostly in north India. The other official Indian language is English.

Hyderabadi:
Anything pertaining to Hyderabad, India

Iftar:
Dinner held to break the daily dawn-to-dusk fast during the Muslim month of Ramadan

Imam:
Islamic religious leader, a Muslim pastor

InshaAllah:
Arabic, meaning "God willing." Also spelled Inshallah

Kachnaal:
A flowering tree found in parts of Pakistan. The flower buds are cooked with spices and the dish is considered a delicacy.

Lota:
Literally, a water pitcher used to wash after a bowel movement. The term is used to denote a turncoat or someone who changes political loyalty for personal gain.

Mayo Clinic:
The world-renowned medical center in Rochester, Minnesota

Mullah:
Urdu, Persian, and Pashtu term for Imam

Paraneoplastic syndrome:
A near fatal condition where body produces excessive amounts
of antibodies to attack cancer. The antibodies then start attacking
healthy organs, particularly the brain.

Pashtu:
An Indo-European language spoken in western Pakistan and
eastern Afghaniatan

Prostatectomy:
Surgical operation to remove prostate gland

Qura'n:
Sacred text that Muslims believe is the word of God, communicated
to Prophet Muhammad through Archangel Gabriel. Also spelled
Quran, Qur'an, or Koran.

Ramadan:
The ninth Muslim month where a complete fast from food and
water is observed from dawn to dusk. The dates for Ramadan move
backwards eleven days each year, and are based on a lunar calendar.

Sahib:
An honorific, like Honorable or Mister

Salaam, salaams:
Abbreviation of Assalamu Alaykum

Sehra:
Literally, a flower veil covering the face of a groom at the time
of wedding. In common use, a Sehra is a wedding poem

Urdu:
An Indo-European language widely spoken in Pakistan and parts
of India

PLACES MENTIONED

Dir:
Mountainous area in north Pakistan

Doha:
Capital of the Persian Gulf state of Qatar

Hayatabad:
City in southern India

Islamabad:
Capital of Pakistan

Mecca:
Birthplace of Islam in Saudi Arabia, where Muslims go for Hajj or pilgrimage

Nithiagali:
A charming small town, a hill station, in Pakistan's Himalayas located about fixty miles northwest of Islamabad. In 1972, during a visit to Pakistan, Henry Kissinger feigned illness and was persuaded by then Pakistani president Yahya Khan to go to Nathiagali to recuperate for a few days. While the press and other American officials waited in Islamabad for Kissinger to come down from the mountain, he had stolen off, in the middle of the night, on a special Pakistan International plane to China for a first-ever official contact between the United States and Communist China.

Puerto Vallarta:
City on the western coast of Mexico

NOTE ABOUT THE AUTHOR

 A 1962 graduate of Khyber Medical College, Peshawar, Pakistan, Dr. Amjad Hussain holds an emeritus professorship in thoracic and cardiovascular surgery at the University of Toledo where he is a member of the University's Board of Trustees.

He is also an explorer, photographer, and writer. Since 1987, he has led four expeditions to explore and photograph the entire 2,200 miles of Indus River in Tibet and Pakistan. *Indus River: Journey of a Lifetime*, a documentary of his Team Indus Expeditions, was shown on PBS stations across the U.S. in April 2005. The documentary can be viewed online at http://www.wgte.org/wgte/watch/item.asp?item_id=98.

Dr. Hussain has served as president of the Islamic Center of Greater Toledo, president of the Academy of Medicine of Toledo, and president of the Toledo Surgical Society. He is a founding member of the Association of Pakistani Physicians of North America and founder of the Khyber Medical College Alumni Association of North America.

For over thirty years he has returned to Peshawar to teach at his alma mater. In recognition of his services, Khyber Medical College awarded him the Lifetime Achievement Award in 2005 and declared him one of the best graduates of the college. In 2012, the college named its newly established Clinical Skills Center after him.

Dr. Hussain has been a columnist on the op-ed pages of The (Toledo) Blade newspaper since 1994. He also writes for a number of other U.S. and Pakistani newspapers. He is the author of six Urdu and six English books on subjects such as culture, history, religion, international relations, and the exploration of the Indus River.

While his literary repertoire is vast, he is best known as the chronicler of life in the old walled city of Peshawar where he was born and raised. In 1998, the governor of Khyber Pukhtunkhwa Province, on behalf of citizens of the city, bestowed on him the title of *Baba-e-Peshawar* (Father of Peshawar) for his efforts to preserve and record the cultural and linguistic legacy of the ancient city.

In 2010, the University of Toledo established an endowed professorship in Thoracic and Cardiovascular Surgery in his name. The University has also created an annual visiting Lectureship in the History of Medicine that carries his name. His other honors include Lifetime Achiever Award of Toledo Press Club, induction into the Medical Mission Hall of Fame, and Communication and Leadership Award of Toastmasters International.

In his spare time—which he claims to have plenty of—Dr. Hussain plays squash racquets, bikes, performs marriages, and does tombstone calligraphy for the Muslim cemetery in Toledo.

ALSO BY S. AMJAD HUSSAIN

The Frontier Town of Peshawar: A Brief History. Silk Road Books. 1993.

Yuk Shehere Arzoo (A City of My Dreams), in Urdu. 1995. Winner of the Abasin Literary Award

Of Home and Country: Journey of a Native Son. Literary Circle of Toledo. 1998.

Aalam Mein Intikhab: Peshawar. (Peshawar: One and Only in the World), in Urdu. Literary Circle of Toledo. 1999.

Mati Ka Qarz (The Debt of the Land), in Urdu. 2000.

The Taliban and Beyond. BWD Publishers. 2001

Citra(N) Wala Katora (A Book of Profiles), in Urdu. 2003.

Dar-e-Maktab (My Journey Through Institutions), in Urdu. Literary Circle of Toledo. 2006.

Treading a Fine Line. Long Riders' Guild Press. 2010.

Shehvani Urdu Shairi (Erotic Urdu Poetry). In Urdu. 2011.

COLLABORATIVE WORKS

The First 150 Years: A History of Academy of Medicine of Toledo, 1851-2001. With Barbara Floyd and Vicki L. Kroll. Literary Circle of Toledo. 2001.

Riding the Fence Lines. With Bernie Keating, Paul Gordon, Michael Kelly, Joel P. Miller, and Seigen Yamaoka. BWD Publishers. 2001.

APPNA Qissa: A History of the Association of Pakistani Physicians of North America, with Barbara Floyd. 2004.

INDEX OF NAMES

Aapa (Umatallah Gulbadshah) 1, 7, 19-20, 33 52, 77, 100, 219
Aapa Gul and Nazir [Hussain] 33
Abdul, Karim 135
Abu-Absi, Samir vi, 163
Adappa, Vijay 53
Adrabi, Imran 81
Adray, Amy 105
Adray, Jim 40, 159
Ahmad, Munir 40, 159
Ahmed, Naveed and Rehana v, 4, 8-9, 18, 31, 37, 40, 77, 81, 83-4,
    86, 107, 112, 116, 128, 130, 135, 137, 157-8
Ahmad, Shamshad 145
Ahmad, Shuaib 14
Ahmed, Noor 105
Ahmed, Siraj and Munawar 15-16, 23, 74, 76-7, 79-81, 135
Akram, Fazle 103
Ali, Imran 73, 81
Ali, Mohsin and Dolores 106, 120
Anand, Satyapal 122
Ashraf, Nasim and Aseela 18, 120
Athar, Shaid 74
Atiq, Omar 92
Awan, Zahoor 17

Baker, Ann 98, 116, 153, 217
Barden, Tom vi, 163
Beego 13-15, 120, 132, 144-5, 152
Begum, (Khursheed) Sheeda 33
Biland, Jill and Bakht 18-19, 66, 73
Biland, Anwar, Sara 73
Black, Kevin (Tasha's husband) 14, 38, 44, 53, 77, 87, 90, 92, 94,
    111-2, 129, 152, 157
Black, Kevin (Tasha's son) 11, 44, 52-3, 87, 92, 94, 117, 152, 158
Black, Tasha (Natasha) iv, 6, 8, 11-12, 21, 31, 37, 40, 42-5, 52-3,
    59, 64, 67, 76-7, 80-2, 86-90, 92-4, 99-101, 107-08, 110-12, 116,

124, 127, 129-31, 138-9, 147, 151, 157
Blanchard, Jim 28
Block, John 2, 105, 120
Brown, Al 8, 81
Brown, Kim and Tony Glinke 11, 34, 77, 116, 124
Burket, Mark 159
Butt, Imtiaz 59

Carrol, Tom 28
Chablani, Lachman and Nanci 8-9, 38, 55, 153
Chablani, Raj and Alisha 8
Chaudhary, Nawaz (Nick) 40, 94-5, 115, 159
Chenevert, Melodie 108, 115
Close, H.M. 121, 132
Corbin, Don 35
Cowie, Ron 50-1, 87, 101, 147
Cubberly, Sue 124

Daniels, Jeff 116
Delagrade, Henry 41, 128
Delagrade, Mary 41-2
Durrani, Farzand Ali 143

Ehsan, Mohsin and Sarwat 130
Emch, Jim 75, 88
Engler, Hannah (Tasha's daughter) v, 6, 9, 11-12, 21, 30, 40, 42-6, 52, 55, 57, 59-60, 77, 80, 88-9, 92, 111, 117, 129, 131, 151, 158, 166, 174

Farooki, Naveed 84
French, Diana 98

Gill, Sukhwinder and Satwant 8-9
Ghafoor, Waheeda 22

Godwin, Lacy 28
Gold, Jeff 77
Greenfield, John and Holly 81
Grubb, Blair 8-9

Haines, Bob 28
Haq, Anwar 27
Hofstadler, Douglas 58
Howard, Dr. and Mrs. John 45, 136
Hussain, Ashfaq and Zahid 17
Hussain, Monie (Osman) iv, 6, 11, 39, 45-6, 51-2, 67, 74, 76-8, 85,
    89-90, 94, 97, 101, 105-7, 111, 115-16, 118-
    120, 127, 139, 152, 158, 173
Hussain, Qarie (Waqaar) iv, 6, 30, 39, 45-6, 51-2, 67, 76-7, 85, 90,
    94, 97, 101-2, 106, 108, 111, 121, 127, 129,
    147, 152, 158, 199
Hussain, Rifaat 59-60

Islam, Mahjabeen 4-5

Jabarin, Saleh 38, 133, 137
Jacobs, Lloyd 77, 115, 129
Javed, Arshad and Saadia 103

Kadri, Cherrefe 77
Kamal, Daud 121
Khalil, Zahid 93
Khan, Abida 9
Khan, Alaf 6, 51, 103, 135
Khan, Hashim 65
Khan, Nasir 88
Khan, Wakil and Abida 94
Khan, Warda 94
Khwaja, David 85, 97

Koko Jan 26, 145
Mahajan, Kewal 7, 125
Mahmood, Marge 30
Marsa, Marcine and Jerry 38
Marshall, Sue and Don 38
Mattoni, John and Linda 136
McCormick, Patrick 38
McEllwine, Calvin 106
Milde, Sylvia 29
Milstead, Jeri 98, 116
Mir, Johar 47
Moran, Garry 89
Morley, Bill and Karen 72
Munawar, Sara (Mona) 118

Naqi, Susie 45
Nazir, Pinchi (Suhail) and Humaira 7
Novack, Rebecca 158

O'Leary, Joe and Ann 48

Pansky, Ben 70
Pirzada, Noor 46, 81
Planks, Max and Sherry 116
Podratz, Karl 73

Rafeeq, Razi and Shahida 4, 77
Rahman, Munib and Zeba 70, 91
Ramnath, Suresh 32
Rasheed, Salman 119
Reed, Ben 153
Reed, Penny 38, 89, 153
Rehan, Arshad 73
Rowlands, Sue Ott 89

Shah, Jafar and Trish 4
Shah, Mustafa 119
Shah, Zubair Ali 15, 31
Shaikh, Bahu 40, 159
Shapiro, Ron 129
Shelbourne, Pauline and Tony 97, 102
Shousher, Hussien and Randa 77
Shousher, Yehia 9
Siddiqui, Atiq 47
Sookie 150
Spooner, Jack and Jill 149
Sternfield, Bill 38

Talmage, Dee and Lance 38
Thaxton, Lara and Kevin 38

Rehman, Maseeh and Tabinda 81

Wealton, Lee 38
Wehabi, Arbid 107
Welch, Corrine and Tom 38
Wolf, Bob and Karen 136

Zafar, Karim 40, 159
Zafar, Saeed 65